BEHIND ENEMY LINES
American Spies and Saboteurs in World War II

This is the story of the Office of Strategic Services and its agents during World War II. All the exciting, dangerous missions that took place in North Africa, Europe, the Far East are recreated from government files that were once stamped confidential but were recently declassified. Now it is possible to read of the danger and intrigue, and feel the atmosphere in which the spy and saboteur existed— the threat of capture, torture, and death just moments away. With the experience gained by the OSS during the war, the seeds were sown for a permanent United States intelligence organization—the Central Intelligence Agency.

BOOKS BY MILTON J. SHAPIRO

Behind Enemy Lines

American Spies and Saboteurs in World War II

Milton J. Shapiro

JULIAN MESSNER NEW YORK

Designed by Miriam Temple

Manufactured in the United States of America

Library of Congress Cataloging in Publication Data

Shapiro, Milton J
  Behind enemy lines.

  Bibliography: p.185
  Includes index.
  1.   World War, 1939–1945—Secret service—United
States—Juvenile literature.   2.   United States.
Office of Strategic Services—Juvenile literature.
I.   Title.
D810.S7S44   940.54'86'73   77–25527
ISBN 0–671–32830–1 lib. bdg.

CONTENTS

1

ACKNOWLEDGMENTS

In the National Archives Building in Washington, D.C., there is a section devoted to the wartime records of the OSS—the Office of Strategic Services. The area needed to keep these files is about the size of the average small town public library. There are thousands and thousands of documents, including original field reports from OSS agents who worked behind enemy lines in World War II. The files are kept behind locked doors. Much of the material is still classified. But a substantial amount of material previously stamped confidential or top secret was recently declassified. The author was privileged to be given access to that material. The greater portion of *Behind Enemy Lines* is derived from those original OSS files and from the OSS history prepared by the U.S. Government Printing Office.

An historian could literally spend years researching in the original OSS field reports. They make fascinating reading. Between the lines of the dry prose used by OSS agents in transmitting, via radio or via courier, the results of their work, it is possible to read of the danger, and the intrigue. It is possible to project the atmosphere in which the spy and the saboteur existed—the threat of capture, torture, and death always just a breath away.

These agents, heroes all, did their work anonymously, operating under code names. Many of them remain anonymous to this day and will forever remain anonymous. Even the declassified OSS files do not reveal their true identities. In some cases, through further research, the author has been able to tie together code names and real names; in such cases, both names are given in the book.

The author wishes to thank John E. Taylor, librarian at the Military Archives Division, for his patience and help in a most taxing job of research. I would also comment on Mr. Taylor's remarkable memory, which on occasion was able to produce, with near magical swiftness, a much needed file in answer to the author's questions.

Thanks are also due Ms. Lynn D. Gunn-Smith, of the Office, Chief of Information, Department of the Army, for her usual help in organizing source material and leads for the author's research.

Some background material for this book and specific details of certain OSS operations were derived from previously published sources. A selected bibliography is included.

Milton J. Shapiro

BEHIND ENEMY LINES

INTRODUCTION

When World War II began in September 1939, the United States had no substantial Intelligence Service. The Army and the Navy each had a handful of men in "Intelligence," some of them cryptographers, some of them career officers shunted into intelligence work when too old or too inefficient for more active duty. Few of these officers spoke a foreign language; fewer still had a gift or a desire for intelligence work.

Europe and the Far East had long standing traditions of intrigue, of espionage. The United States, isolationist after the First World War, with no enemies on its borders, had little need or regard for the romantic cloak-and-dagger "game" of spying, as portrayed in films and works of fiction.

There was one American, however, who was more alert than most to the threat of Nazi Germany, to the threat of a global war that would involve the United States. This man, Maj. Gen. William "Wild Bill" Donovan, also saw that in modern warfare all the rules had changed. He saw that unconventional warfare would play an important role in years to come. He saw that special operations, within the framework of a sophisticated Intelligence system, could be as important a weapon against an enemy as several divisions in the field.

Donovan was a colorful, complicated man with a tremendous ego. He was a "doer," and because of the drive of his ego and his vision, he rubbed many people the wrong way. Fortunately for the United States, and for the Intelligence organization he was to head, Donovan's manner of doing things was precisely what this country needed when the Japanese bombed Pearl Harbor on December 7, 1941, and hurtled America headlong into the war.

By that time, Donovan was almost ready for it.

Donovan got his name "Wild Bill" playing football for Columbia University—or so legend has it. Some say he won the name as a heroic, dashing Colonel with the famous Fighting Irish 69th Division in World War I. He won the Medal of Honor during the fighting in the Meuse-Argonne campaign. In any case, he was known everywhere as "Wild Bill." It was a nickname he did not discourage.

After the war Donovan became a lawyer and dabbled a bit in politics. But he had a hobby—war. Donovan chased wars the way some people chase fire engines. Usually as an "interested" private citizen, but sometimes as a "semi-official" government observer, Donovan traveled the world covering the fighting fronts. He went to

Manchuria in 1931, to Ethiopia in 1935 to watch Benito Mussolini's first venture into conquest, and to Spain after that to observe the bloody Civil War and watch Nazi Germany test some of its new weapons in support of Franco.

When Donovan came back from Ethiopia and from Spain, he bluntly aired his views on the new look of modern warfare, views which often as not conflicted with some of the stodgy thinking found among staff officers of both the Army and Navy. When Donovan spoke of spies and saboteurs, of propaganda agents working for the Fascists and the Nazis, when he tried to alert the Congress and the people to the dangers he saw, he was put down as a "scare-monger."

Most Americans, quite understandably, did not want to become involved in what they saw as a coming "European War." Bitter memories of World War I were still too fresh in too many minds. Donovan was seen as an "interventionist" who was eager to send American boys overseas to be killed.

Time and time again in his speeches, President Franklin D. Roosevelt avowed that he did not intend to send American boys overseas into another war. But the President knew, as Donovan and many others close to the White House knew, that sooner or later, if a full-scale war broke out in Europe, the United States would become involved—voluntarily or otherwise.

In August 1940, with the war almost a year old in Europe, France fallen, Great Britain under savage air attack by the Luftwaffe, and Hitler's Nazi Germany riding the crest of military victory, Donovan journeyed to

Washington to testify before Congress on the pending
Military Training Bill.

Suddenly, Donovan was called to the White House,
summoned personally by President Roosevelt. The President had a secret mission for him. He was to go to
Britain and report on what he found there. The President wanted Donovan's firsthand observations on the
war and on Britain's state of morale and military
strength. He wanted Donovan to find out all he could
about Nazi spies, saboteurs, and propagandists and how
they had worked so successfully in Europe.

Donovan returned much impressed with British
morale and courage. He returned, too, with a tremendous amount of information, not only on the German Intelligence Services, but on British Intelligence as
well. He told the President and his aides that the British
were years ahead of us in Intelligence operations. He
predicted that in the months and years ahead the use of
Intelligence and special operations would play an ever
increasing role in the strategies of both Britain and Germany. He advised that our own Intelligence system be
completely reorganized and modernized.

Donovan made another point; he said that the Mediterranean area would soon become an area of paramount
importance to both sides in the war, and that this area
must be kept open as a communications and supply life-
line.

President Roosevelt not only agreed with this thinking, he sent Donovan off to the Mediterranean to scout
out the area. For more than three months Donovan
studied the strategic implications of the Mediterranean

theater of war, right on the spot, observing, talking, but mostly listening—to the British, to the locals, to anybody who knew anything about the Mediterranean.

When he returned once again to the White House, he told of the new British commando units, of small task-force teams specially trained and equipped to hit and run, to strike at specific enemy targets and get out, to commit sabotage, and to train and lead guerrilla units behind enemy lines. He told, too, of the increase in espionage and propaganda warfare practiced by both the British and the Germans in the countries of the Mediterranean.

President Roosevelt was tremendously impressed. He immediately appointed a high-level Cabinet committee to examine Donovan's reports and to decide on a course of action. Two months later, on July 11, 1941, an Executive Order signed by President Roosevelt created the Office of Coordinator of Information. Donovan was its chief.

Because the United States was still a neutral country, the words used to create Donovan's job had to be diplomatically chosen; there could be no references to enemies, or war, or espionage, or intelligence activities. Donovan's job was the collection of "information and data which bear upon national security."

Five months later, while Donovan was still organizing the COI and recruiting staff, Pearl Harbor changed everything, including the official scope of his department. In January 1942, President Roosevelt called Donovan to his office once again. This time the President bluntly told Donovan that he was to organize a vast new

Intelligence network along the lines of the British SOE—Special Operations Executive. (Donovan already had a COI operation functioning in London.)

"Bill," the President said to him gravely, "you will have to begin with nothing. We have no Intelligence Service."

On June 13, 1942, President Roosevelt issued a new Executive Order, changing the Office of Coordinator of Information to the Office of Strategic Services—the OSS, soon to be called in Washington, the "Oh, So Secret."

The responsibilities of the OSS were widened to include "such special services as may be directed by the United States Joint Chiefs of Staff."

This reference to "special services" put a whole new face on Donovan's job. His area of operations now included the entire world except for a specific area in the Pacific, the Far Eastern Command, where Gen. Douglas MacArthur refused to permit operations by the OSS. And now, for the first time in the history of the United States, a sophisticated Intelligence agency, *one* agency, was the umbrella under which all intelligence collection would operate. Additionally, this agency, the OSS, had the task of coordinating counterintelligence (except in the United States and in South America, covered by the FBI), supporting resistance movements in countries occupied by the Germans, the Italians, and the Japanese, organizing acts of sabotage, commando-type missions, and psychological warfare—and doing just about anything else the regular armed forces of the United States could not, or were not prepared to, do.

At the height of the war, the OSS would number some

twelve thousand, with perhaps another ten thousand "free-lance" men and women in foreign countries working on special assignments, often as "one-offs."

Donovan recruited a strange assortment of personalities to launch his OSS. But then, the OSS was a strange kind of organization, attracting and needing an unusual kind of person—a person who could play a strange, and most dangerous, kind of game.

Donovan needed people with a wide range of skills—fluency in foreign languages, knowledge of foreign countries, and expertise with explosives and weapons, radio equipment, cameras, and printing equipment. He needed people with social and business contacts all over the world. He needed experts in finance, in agriculture, in mapmaking. He needed people who knew every alleyway in Naples, Paris, Berlin, and Casablanca; people who knew the cost of a train ticket from Trieste to Milan, or from Cairo to Damascus. Trivial details were vital to an agent in the field, and what Donovan needed more than anything was people who had this kind of knowledge.

So a strange collection of personalities flocked around "Wild Bill" Donovan in the early days of the OSS. Many of them, for the reasons stated above, were foreign-born, intensely loyal Americans; some of them refugees from Fascism and Nazism. There were actors, bankers, lawyers, college professors, athletes—and more than a few reformed safecrackers and master forgers.

One of the greatest forgers—or rather, one of the most notorious forgers—of all time, known as "Jim the Penman," worked for the OSS. He forged hundreds of

Gestapo and SS orders and documents for agents working in Europe. He became a master at forging the signature of Heinrich Himmler, Chief of the SS (*Schutzstaffel* —Hitler's élite corps of troopers).

In the beginning, there was no one to teach these recruits how to carry out their difficult and dangerous tasks of espionage and sabotage. There were no teachers and there was no time. It was understood that mistakes would be made, and that there would be casualties, sometimes heavy casualties. Every agent knew that to be caught in civilian clothes in an act of espionage or sabotage meant probable execution—there was no prisoner-of-war status where there was no uniform.

The OSS was organized into several distinct departments. There were Secret Intelligence, Special Operations, and Research and Analysis, to begin with; later Morale Operations was added, then Counter-Espionage, a Maritime Unit, Research and Development, and a Medical Service.

Special Operations and Secret Intelligence were the two "glamorous" sections. Donovan found no shortage of recruits for them, though they were, of course, the two most dangerous ones. In some ways the two departments overlapped, but their original strategic concepts were different.

Donovan himself thought of Special Operations as a quasi-military department, directing commando strikes and large-scale sabotage operations and cooperating with existing guerrilla groups behind enemy lines, in the occupied countries. When the war ended, Special Operations would end.

On the other hand, Secret Intelligence was considered to be of longer-range interest, a department that might well remain intact after the war, giving the United States a permanent Intelligence organization.

The function of an agent in Secret Intelligence was to root out information that could be of any use at all, directly or indirectly. For example, knowledge that the price of bread in Berlin had gone sky-high would be useful, because it would indicate shortages in supplies in Germany and possible lowering of morale of the German people. Of more direct value would be the movements of troop trains, the shifting of a general from one area to another, the locations of tank factories, and so forth. Sometimes information gathered might seem trivial, and sometimes information secured by an agent was momentous enough to alter the course of the war, to save thousands of lives.

These agents, the clandestine "trench-coated spy" of fiction, operated under many different "cover" situations. In neutral countries they posed as businessmen, journalists, tourists, playboys, smugglers, and what have you. In many cases these agents worked under the cover of diplomatic status out of a United States Embassy or Consulate office. Agents were needed in neutral countries, such as Switzerland, Portugal, Spain, and Sweden, to provide a chain of stations for the passage of information, via radio or courier. They also kept watch on suspected enemy agents, spied out information on the flow of trade goods to the enemy via the neutral country, and used their bases to recruit, train, and pay other agents in the field.

Operating in enemy territory was another matter entirely. Here the agent had to blend into the background
and observe every caution. The Germans, our prime
enemy in Europe, had many levels of counterintelligence, all of them clever and ruthless. Agents, sometimes
operating in the country of their birth, sought out help
among courageous citizens, who risked torture and death
by housing and aiding the OSS men, feeding them,
acting as couriers, and spying for them.

In short order, as Donovan recruited, trained as best
he could, and then sent them on their missions, OSS
agents were at work in Africa, France, Italy, Germany;
indeed, throughout Europe and the Middle East.
Dropped by plane, landed by rubber raft, penetrating by
foot, car, train, and even bicycle, OSS agents by the
hundreds, then by the thousands, took up their work as
spies, saboteurs, radio operators, guerrilla leaders. They
sent back to their control points, to their mission chiefs,
an incredible amount of intelligence. They blew up
bridges, supply trains, and factories; they killed enemy
soldiers, tied up thousands more hunting them down,
and, in one most spectacular case, helped bring about
the surrender of complete German armies (see Operation Sunrise).

The nature of the war in the Pacific did not lend itself
to the same kind of intelligence-gathering operations.
There Special Operations dominated the tactics of the
OSS. Agents worked with guerrilla movements fighting
the Japanese and found themselves allied with resistance
leaders such as Ho Chi Minh and Mao Tse-tung. OSS
field reports on Ho and Mao, and on the revolutionary

movements in Vietnam and China, made for "hot" reading in Washington during the war. Some of those reports will be found in the chapters on the Far East.

In Burma, OSS Special Operations agents led native Kachin tribesmen in a constant war of harassment against the Japanese, operating completely behind the enemy lines at all times.

There are a thousand true adventure stories in the files of the OSS. Within the pages of one book it would be impossible to do justice to the exploits of individual agents. The purpose in *Behind Enemy Lines*, therefore, is to paint a broader picture, to give the reader a historical view of the OSS and the part it played in World War II, highlighting some of the more important missions and operations.

NORTH AFRICA:
Operation Torch

North Africa was the testing ground for the newly created OSS. In January 1942, when it was still called the Office of Coordinator of Information, the organization began placing agents in Algeria and French Morocco, where the British were excluded. The agents were briefed to gather intelligence and prepare sabotage units in the event of a German invasion of French North Africa and to recruit help from locals sympathetic to the Allied cause in support of American landings scheduled for the months ahead. The American landings, originally scheduled for April 1942, were codenamed Operation Torch.

To understand why the British were not welcome in French North Africa, it is necessary to go back to events of 1940. The German *Blitzkrieg* in the spring of 1940 forced France to surrender; technically, the French concluded an Armistice with the Germans. The British forces evacuated France and returned to defend their island against a German invasion that never came.

As part of the Franco-German Armistice, Hitler left a large area of southern France unoccupied—called Vichy France after its capital city. Similarly, French North Africa remained nominally French, though of course controlled by Frenchmen who agreed to take orders from Berlin.

As far as the British were concerned, French leaders who collaborated with the Germans were enemies. They wanted the French Admirals to scuttle their fleet in North African ports, rather than allow the ships and ports to be used by Germans. When the French declined, the British Navy attacked the French in July 1940, at Mers El Kebir and at Dakar. This closed French North Africa to British activity. All British nationals were banned from the area. Their diplomatic and intelligence personnel were restricted to an area in the international city of Tangier, Morocco, overlooking the Straits of Gibraltar.

Into the vacuum left by the British Secret Intelligence Service (SIS) moved COI/OSS. The Americans were not yet in the war and were free to move about. In actual fact, as early as February 1941, partly as a result of Donovan's urging, a certain amount of intelligence gathering had been underway. At that time, the U.S. State Department concluded an economic agreement with Gen. Maxime Weygand, Commander of Vichy French forces in North Africa.

As part of the agreement, twelve vice-consuls were sent to North Africa, presumably to check on shipments of food, cotton, and petroleum. They were given access to ports and permission to inspect outgoing ships, since the agreement specified that U.S. imports were not to be transshipped to Germany or Italy.

These twelve vice-consuls were actually selected by the Intelligence departments of the Army and Navy and briefed on intelligence activities. The vice-consuls proceeded to gather information on German and Vichy-French defenses and military activities and aided a number of British agents hampered by their restriction to Tangier. One vice-consul agreed to act as paymaster for the British SIS in Tangier, handling payments for local agents in the field. Another provided a wireless transmitter for a British agent who needed regular contact with the British on the island of Malta. In Casablanca, the vice-consul worked for the British SIS as a liaison agent until the American landings in November 1942.

All twelve vice-consuls came under control of the OSS Station Chief in January 1942. From that point on, the United States being a belligerent nation, American agents were in the same boat as the British—enemies of the Germans, the Italians, and the pro-Nazi French. The job of the American agents now became more than just a matter of routine intelligence gathering. There were added other aspects of an agent's brief: subversion, resistance, sabotage. On the propaganda front, agents were directed to gain the cooperation of as many French as they could, in anticipation of the forthcoming invasion. More directly, they were to penetrate and try to subvert units of the French Fascist organizations in North Africa, the SOL and the PPF (Service d'Ordre Legionnaire, which was a veterans' organization, and the Parti Populaire Français).

One of the first things the new station chief did when he arrived in January 1942 was organize the existing agency system onto a wartime footing. At the time, two each of the vice-consuls/agents were operating out of Tunis, Oran, and Algiers, with the remaining six in Casablanca. The station chief chose six of the ablest of the vice-consuls and a regular State Department vice-consul with ten years' experience and set them up in a new communications network. Tangier was to be the new control point, instead of Washington.

Frenchmen sympathetic to the Allied cause who had radio experience were then recruited, sent secretly to Gibraltar to be trained by the British, and then returned to await proper equipment. By July 1942, five clandestine radio stations were in operation, codenamed Midway (the Algiers base station), Lincoln (Casablanca), Yankee (Algiers), Pilgrim (Tunis), and Franklin (Oran).

The existence of these radio stations was ultrasecret. Nobody in the U.S. State Department or any other department knew of their existence. Thus, the American invasion plans for North Africa were known to just a handful of personnel and remained secret up to H-Hour.

French North Africa in 1942 was a peculiar place, and, because of its bizarre position, was often the locale of spy thrillers in books and films (*Casablanca*, with Humphrey Bogart and Ingrid Bergman instantly springs to mind). The area was neither completely neutral nor actually a belligerent. Americans were allowed in the area, but denied access to such sensitive locations as docks and airfields. At the same time, under the terms of the Franco-German Armistice of 1940, Germans and

Italians had access everywhere. On the surface, these
Axis personnel were supposed to be economists, agricul-
tural experts, military "advisors," and so forth. In reality,
most of them were Gestapo or Intelligence agents, and
they spent a good deal of their time matching wits with
the American agents. Because nobody at that point
wanted to be accused of violating Vichy French sov-
ereignty—such as it was—the game went on with a
maximum of maneuvering and a minimum of violence.

Of constant concern to the Allied planners of Operation Torch was a German flanking attack through Spain
and into North Africa. There was little confidence that
Franco, the pro-German Spanish dictator, would resist
such a German thrust through his country. To help prepare for such an attack, two agents, trained in Canada by
British SOE, and with firsthand knowledge of French
and Spanish Morocco, were dispatched to Tangier in
April 1942.

Their special task was to organize resistance groups
among the native population. Neither of the two largest
indigenous groups had any love for the French—their
masters for decades—nor any reason to love the Germans. And so, with money, arms, and persuasion, these
two key agents made a deal with "Strings," the codename for the religious leader of the Moors of North
Morocco, and with "Tassels," codename for the leader of
the Riffs.

Members of the "Strings" group numbered tens of
thousands of Moors ready to obey without question the
orders of their divine leader. Sheiks, holy men, farmers,
and shepherds, penetrating strategic areas forbidden to

outsiders, relayed intelligence information through their religious leaders.

The colorful Riffs from the Atlas Mountains, Berber adventurers portrayed in many an old Foreign Legion film, were old hands at conducting guerrilla warfare in difficult terrain. The French had been battling them for years, never conquering them completely. In recommending their aid, Donovan, in a secret memo to President Roosevelt, pointed out that in putting down a Riff uprising in 1925, the French needed 150,000 men and 30 batteries of artillery.

The two OSS agents handling "Strings" and "Tassels" had to be extremely careful. Because of ancient tribal rivalries, it was vital that neither native leader knew of the other's cooperation, or the entire deal would be off. Thus meetings were held at constantly shifting rendezvous, as much to avoid friendly spying as to avoid Gestapo agents.

Under OSS tutelage, and armed via Gibraltar with British Sten guns, .45 pistols, rifles, and explosives, the Moslem and Riff groups were formed into cells for sabotage and resistance. An ambitious plan was also formulated, calling for a major uprising by 80,000 natives against the Vichy French, should the Germans attack through Spain.

As D-Day for Operation Torch approached, OSS agents began to smuggle out of North Africa key people who could help the planners with technical details. This was done by hiding them on Portuguese fishing boats plying between Casablanca and Lisbon, or on British boats going from Tangier to Gibraltar. One agent got an important harbor pilot out by hiding him in the trunk of his car as he drove from Port Lyautey to Tangier. This pilot's services with the invasion on D-Day won him a Silver Star and a Navy Cross.

On October 22, OSS agents, Ambassador Robert Murphy, and cooperative French military leaders met at Cherchell Beach (seventy-five miles from Algiers) with Gen. Mark Clark, secretly landed by submarine. At this meeting, final plans for Operation Torch were revealed—except the exact date and places of landing. The American commanders were taking no chances on a last-minute French change of heart.

Rumors of an Allied invasion had been floating around North Africa for several months. Both sides originated and encouraged rumors. The Germans did it, hoping that denials would give them a clue to the truth; the OSS did it to confuse the issue. Cleverly, OSS agents planted enough false trails to convince the Germans that the landings would take place at Dakar. At the same time, agents spread rumors that the British on Malta were starving to death, and that a large food convoy was on its way. This story was told so convincingly that the Germans were completely fooled by the Allied invasion convoy of 150 ships, as it passed through the Straits of Gibraltar.

As D-Day for Torch approached (November 8, 1942), further cover activities were provided. One OSS agent sent out invitations for a party to be given on November 10. Another made elaborate plans for a trip out to the country on the invasion weekend, inviting several friends. Since none of the French or native resistance groups knew the exact invasion date, none could give it away to the anxious Germans by a sudden spurt of activity or other suspicious behavior.

Security was almost too good, in fact. The invasion proved to be such a surprise that a number of resistance leaders were away from their posts and could not be contacted in time to carry out their missions.

But the OSS, in this, its first major test, did its paramount job. Deception was complete. While more than 100,000 Allied troops waded ashore over a stretch of some 2,000 miles of North African coastline, seven squadrons of Sicily-based Luftwaffe bombers and fighters circled the Mediterranean 300 miles to the east, searching in vain for the Malta-bound food convoy.

On the beaches, U.S. troops were met by friendly guides. Resistance by a few surprised Vichy French Army and Navy groups was minimal. The invasion forces came ashore armed with accurate maps; they knew the disposition of the French fleet, the numbers of planes on every airfield, the locations of antiaircraft and artillery batteries, the locations of the Germans and the Italians in the invasion area, and who the friends were among the French.

To the doubters among military commanders, the work of the OSS in preparation for Operation Torch was a revelation. Gen. George C. Marshall, in command of Allied forces, commended the OSS in a letter to Gen. Donovan.

The OSS had passed its first test with flying colors.

But there were some deadly pitfalls waiting just over the horizon.

One month after the Allied landings in North Africa, the first OSS secret agent team penetrated enemy-held Europe. This was effected by a Frenchman, codenamed "Tommy," who was a radio operator on the Operation Torch OSS team. Because of his connections with the French Intelligence section, the Deuxième Bureau, Tommy was asked to organize a team which would set up a clandestine radio and direct intelligence on the island of Corsica.

Tommy obtained a Deuxième Bureau officer and three native Corsicans as assistants and then wangled a submarine out of the French Navy in Algiers. On December 11, 1942, the five agents, loaded with three wireless sets, French francs, Italian lire, food, supplies, Sten guns, and pistols, boarded the submarine *Casablanca* and set out for Corsica.

This was the first such mission ever tried, and the technique used by Capt. l'Herminier, the submarine commander, became the standard for all future missions of this type. Upon reaching the target area, he made a daylight periscope reconnaissance until a suitable landing spot was found, a deserted beach at the foot of the Bay of Chioni. The Captain then submerged and held the submarine on the bottom until after dark.

Only an expert submarine commander—and a gutsy one—could manage such a feat. It required detailed knowledge of the underwater conditions in the area and masterful maneuvering. Then, shortly after midnight on December 14, the *Casablanca* resurfaced, hull barely out of the water to avoid being seen by shore patrols and moved to within a mile of the beach. Two crew members then landed the agents and their equipment by dinghy.

The submarine then resubmerged and returned to its position for thirty hours. At that point a second boatload of supplies was to be sent ashore and agent Tommy brought back to the sub. But on this second trip, the dinghy capsized. The two crewmen were stranded on shore and remained with the OSS group for two months, until another submarine arrived with supplies and rescued them.

Tommy, ordered to return to Algiers for another briefing, did return to the *Casablanca* by swimming for an hour and a half in the treacherous waters of the bay.

On December 25, Christmas Day, the Corsica station, codenamed Pearl Harbor, transmitted its first message back to Algiers. They reported that the Italians had an occupying force of some 25,000 men on the island, backed up by a small force of Germans. The Corsicans, with a history of fierce love of liberty and independence, hated the Italians and welcomed the OSS team, pledging complete cooperation.

It was on Corsica that the word "maquis" was first applied to underground resistance fighters. Later, the word was applied generally to all French resistance groups. But the first "maquis" were the Corsican Maquis, who took the name from the high, dense shrubbery, called maquis, which covers the sides of the Corsican mountains. During the nineteenth century, in the days of the Vendetta when terrible blood feuds raged among Corsican families, the maquis was the traditional hiding place for outcasts.

Unhappily, the Corsican operation suffered from OSS

inexperience and the excess enthusiasm of the Corsicans themselves. Security just did not exist. Corsican families, closely united by blood ties and a contempt for the Italian occupation troops, took no precautions. They spoke openly of their aid to the OSS team and boasted of the day of liberation soon to come. That Station Pearl Harbor lasted for the five months it did was evidence of Italian inefficiency.

In the summer of 1943 the chief radio operator was captured, tortured, and killed. The other members of the team simply disappeared. They were never heard from again. By this time, however, Tommy was not with the group, having been pulled out of Corsica for the next OSS advance into enemy-held territory, France itself.

On the basis of Operation Torch and his successful launch of the Corsican operation, agent Tommy was held in high regard by both the OSS and British Intelligence. Accordingly, when the Germans wiped out a British Special Operations station near Nice, in southern France, Tommy was sent in to set up a new station. At this point in the war, menaced by the American forces in North Africa, the Germans had occupied all the rest of France.

Once again employing the submarine *Casablanca* and the Corsican technique, Tommy landed in the south of France, near Marseilles. Quickly contacting key figures in the underground movement, he helped set up a new clandestine radio station for British Special Operations, another in Marseilles for the French resistance, and a station codenamed Mexico for the OSS near Toulon.

Of necessity Tommy was a one-man OSS band. He

was given virtual independence in the recruitment and training of new OSS agents on the spot and responsibility for security. This abdication of control by OSS headquarters in Algiers led to unfortunate complications later on.

Officially, Tommy was supposed to work in liaison with the French intelligence network known as SR— Services de Renseignements. This group was loyal to General Giraud. But the resistance movements in all the occupied countries were splintered into rival factions. In France, the SR was opposed by patriots who supported Gen. Charles de Gaulle as the leader of the French Government-in-Exile. These resistance fighters helped Tommy set up Mexico, gave him a radio operator, and promised him a network of agents all over the south of France.

Tommy had to become an adept juggler. The rival resistance groups were extremely suspicious of each other—even hostile. Thus, as with Strings and Tassels in North Africa, they had to be kept in ignorance of each other's contact with the OSS. In addition, for security reasons, Tommy had to keep both factions ignorant of his contact with the British SOE station.

Despite all precautions, Tommy's relationship with the three groups was discovered, and bitter jealousy erupted. The reader today might well wonder at this rivalry among resistance and Intelligence groups, when the common goal was the defeat of the Axis powers. But this jockeying for power existed from the smallest resistance units all the way through to generals and the heads of state. Throughout the war, for example, the rivalry between America's Gen. George Patton and Britain's Gen. Bernard Montgomery was notorious. On the highest levels, the United States, Britain, France, and Russia constantly maneuvered for power positions with one eye on postwar alliances and political advantage.

Moreover, many of the resistance groups in Europe were Communist-oriented—some independent, some with definite sympathy and affiliation with Russia. These groups, it must be said, fought hard and fought well against Nazi and Fascist occupation. But these political differences, compounded by personal ambition, often led to the kind of problem the OSS—and agent Tommy—had to cope with.

When the Giraud-backed SR in southern France discovered Tommy's liaison with the de Gaullists, their jealous reaction went beyond normal suspicions and grumblings. Leading officers of the SR actually plotted to blow the whole Mexico apparatus to the Gestapo. This would discredit the de Gaullists and their promises of security and give the SR the leading intelligence role in southern France.

Fortunately, this never came off. But Tommy took no more chances. He established a secondary radio base sixty miles north of Marseilles that the SR knew nothing about. In any case, despite the problems, Tommy proved to be of fantastic value to the OSS. In particular, his messages to Algiers on the movements of enemy ships out of Marseilles led directly to Allied torpedoing of five cargo ships on their way to enemy ports in Tunisia.

Even more spectacular, Tommy obtained the complete disposition of German antiaircraft units in France, including the code warning signal. He got this by bribing a German major with gold obtained from Algiers.

Tommy also sent hundreds of messages with information on troop movements, goods trains, Luftwaffe dispositions, and so forth.

Another blow to Tommy's security came when the newly formed French desk in Algiers decided to send a new group of agents to all three stations in southern France—French, British, and American. They would be sent in by submarine. Tommy was instructed to guide in the submarine by blinker signals at night, get the landing parties organized, and then return on the submarine to Algiers. There he would get new instructions for further missions.

Tommy did not like this. He alone knew the extent of the dangers existing in his area due to rivalries and jealousies. He felt he should remain on the scene. He also resented new men coming into the area without his approval. But, orders were orders.

Back in Algiers, Tommy worked with the new OSS chief there on plans for sending badly needed supplies to southern France. Part of these supplies would be sample U.S. weapons, which would be distributed to resistance groups. Weapons and supplies would be dropped by parachute.

Tommy was to be leader of the supply expedition. He took a parachute course and was made familiar with the use of mortars, machine guns, grenades, and explosives. Then, on the night of June 19, 1943, he flew out of Algiers on a British Halifax and dropped near Mont Ventoux, in the Vercors region, shortly after midnight.

He was met by a Maquis group and set up in the area a new radio station, codenamed Boston. For the next few months Tommy expanded the OSS agent network, arranged for two more supply drops, and set up two additional radio stations, Texas, at Carcassonne, and York, at Toulon.

The Gestapo were not asleep while all this was going on. They were becoming more and more aggressive in their searches for these clandestine radio stations. Finally, an inexperienced agent in Toulon got careless in trying to make contact with station Mexico. He was caught by the Gestapo and killed, and station Mexico was wiped out.

Tommy was now badly shaken. The destruction of station Mexico and the loss of his men came at a time when supply difficulties were causing frustration and loss of support among the Maquis. He needed more money, more food, more guns to keep the expanding network operative. None was forthcoming. OSS Algiers said bad weather was making parachute drops difficult. This was only partially true, however. Algiers was more seriously hampered by the absence of U.S. Army Air Force support. The OSS still depended on the British RAF, and the British were not always ready to lend aircraft to the exclusive OSS operation. In fact, Tommy's initial drop in the Halifax was arranged only because he agreed to take along supplies for a British SOE unit.

Faced with a crisis situation, Tommy set out for Algiers, via Spain. There followed a remarkable journey, on foot, through the Pyrenees Mountains and on into Spain, avoiding German Army patrols and Gestapo checkpoints all the way. Finally Tommy made it to Barcelona, where he reported to the United States Embassy and his OSS contact there. But he got no farther. A message awaited him, along with new codes, signal plans, and a million francs. He was to return at once to southern France. All was in disorder there. Station York had been captured by the Gestapo and the rest of the operation was in danger of extermination.

Tommy was smuggled back over the border into France. He made first for Carcassonne (about fifty miles from the Spanish border), moved the position of station Texas, and changed its codename to Dartmouth. He continued on to station Boston and moved it just minutes before the Gestapo closed in on it for the kill. Thus the two stations were apparently saved, but several of Tommy's most trusted agents were captured—and never heard from again.

Soon afterward, Tommy was ordered back to Algiers. But the best of his work was all behind him. A month later, station Boston went off the air, wiped out by the Gestapo. Then, on November 5, 1943, OSS Algiers detected a strange operator working the radio out of station Dartmouth. They could tell by the difference in his manner of sending over the ticker key. Each operator had a minute difference, as distinguishing as a handwritten signature, in the way he transmitted messages.

Tommy was called in to listen. Yes, he said, this sounded different, but in any case the new operator would have been trained under his orders, by one of his men, and there was nothing to worry about. A week later, when the original Dartmouth operator came back on, it appeared that Tommy's assurances had been warranted.

It took a very long time, almost eighteen months in fact, for the OSS to discover that station Dartmouth was operating under German control. What happened was this: the Gestapo captured Tommy's operator, and for one week replaced him with one of their own men. Using Dartmouth's codebook, the German operator sent a few harmless messages, hoping to pick up information in return about the Allied invasion plans for France. After the week, it was no longer necessary to continue the deception; a week with the Gestapo was long enough to "persuade" the original Dartmouth agent to work under their control.

For nearly a year in southern France, then for six months in Germany when the station was advanced, Dartmouth was under German control. This proved to be the only OSS station throughout the war to be "played back" for such a long period of time without detection. There were three reasons for this German success. First, OSS inexperience in allowing operators to be recruited in the field without ever being briefed on security at the home base. Second, again inexperience, in failing to supply the operators with a prearranged signal for reporting capture. Later this was corrected. For example, when an operator went into the field, he might be told to misspell the word "artillery" each time he sent a message. Then, if he were captured and forced to work under control, he would signal his base to that effect by sending the code word spelled correctly.

Because these procedures were not in use at the time,

Algiers had no reason to suspect the Dartmouth operator once Tommy had dispelled their doubts. The third reason for the German success was that they played back the station very carefully. Had they picked up OSS agents and Maquis contacts in large numbers soon after capturing Dartmouth, they would have given the game away. But they allowed some agents to continue operations, although under strict surveillance, and, in one instance, let two important members of the French resistance pass through the station.

During its period under German control Dartmouth continued to send Algiers some useful information. The Germans had to do this to keep Dartmouth credible. The information they fed was relatively unimportant, however. At the same time they got in return information from Algiers useful to them. Fortunately none of it was vital. But it did result in casualties. Four two-man teams dropped into southern France at Dartmouth's request were never heard from and were presumed lost to the Gestapo. Since the OSS casualty rate was in any case high in southern France, the Algiers base did not implicate Dartmouth in these losses.

Then, in October 1943, the Dartmouth operator signaled that he had the chance to move into Austria. He explained that with the German withdrawal from the Marseilles area, he would be more useful elsewhere. Algiers agreed. Dartmouth moved to Feldkirch.

From Feldkirch Dartmouth began to send information on German defenses in the area and on the work of native Austrian resistance movements. Later, most of this information proved to be false. Dartmouth remained in business for quite some time in Austria, but eventually fell afoul of the German "overkill" in the area. The Germans were particularly successful in tracking down Allied agents in Austria. British SOE units were being wiped out regularly, and OSS units not connected with Dartmouth ran into similar difficulties. The casualty rate was virtually one hundred percent.

When Dartmouth asked for two agents to be dropped, OSS Algiers thought twice about it, but eventually sent the men. The two-man team dropped right into the arms of the waiting Gestapo. This was now the fifth team lost after being sent to Dartmouth. Combined with the other heavy losses in Austria, this was too much to accept. Dartmouth was now under suspicion again, and all communications with the station cut off. How much Dartmouth was to blame for the other casualties among the OSS in Austria was never discovered.

Tommy did not escape unscathed. He was charged with being a double agent, since Dartmouth was his man, and he had taken great pains to assure Algiers that the operator was trustworthy. His case was not helped by the French SR, which disliked and distrusted him anyway because of his de Gaullist connections. They, too, charged him with being an enemy agent.

To clear himself of the charges, Tommy went to London, by then the focal point of all OSS activity in Europe. In London he was to a large extent cleared of the charges by American and British Intelligence personnel who knew firsthand of his successful and loyal work in the field.

But he was never completely exonerated. Suspicions

remained. Tommy was "retired" as an agent. Even German documents captured at the end of the war indicating that Dartmouth had been compromised by Gestapo "persuasion" failed to clear Tommy completely. Such is the nature of Intelligence work.

Much of all that transpired in southern France, including the high rate of casualties, could be put down to OSS inexperience. In balance, however, the OSS work in North Africa, the Western Mediterranean, and southern France was considered to be first-rate, the intelligence gained and the sabotage perpetrated well worth the loss in men and material.

This can be reasonably defended by the OSS record in these areas, despite Operation Banana—the worst OSS blunder of the war. Operation Banana was launched while Tommy was operating in southern France. It was conceived in Tangier, by OSS, working in conjunction with the U.S. Fifth Army Commander, Gen. Mark Clark.

After the initial success of Operation Torch, the job of protecting the western defenses of North Africa fell to Gen. George Patton's Western Task Force. When Patton moved into Tunisia to take up a combat command, Gen. Clark and Fifth Army moved in. More than just an occupation force, Fifth Army began training for operations against the mainland of Europe. Clark and the Allied commanders were still worried about a German attack on their flank through Spain, and so prepared Operation Backbone, out of which would come Banana.

The Backbone plan included the sending of American armored columns into Spanish Morocco in the event of a

German advance through Spain. In addition, the Strings and Tassels groups were to assist with a major insurrection. Gen. Clark agreed to all this, including arming and paying Strings and Tassels via Fifth Army Headquarters, which was at Oujda.

Aside from military intelligence, Gen. Clark wanted OSS to provide political intelligence. He felt this was necessary, since he trusted neither all the French in North Africa nor all the Arabs. He wanted to know, via OSS, about French officials with Fascist and/or Nazi sympathies and about any Arab organizations which might pose a threat to security. Further, he wanted information about German espionage and sabotage operations throughout North Africa, and, perhaps most important of all, information about any German military preparations going on in Spain.

OSS agents got to work briskly. In short order, they discovered a nest of French civilians and military personnel spying for Germany. This included the commander of the garrison at Fez, in Morocco. Then German and Italian espionage schools at Tetuan, in Spanish Morocco, were discovered and infiltrated. OSS-controlled agents were smuggled across the border to enlist in these schools. One agent came back with a German questionnaire on the American Army and the harbor at Casablanca. A week later he returned to Spanish Morocco with the answers—supplied by OSS, aimed at convincing the Germans with correct-looking, but wrong information. Another agent, Italian-born, penetrated an Italian school in Spanish Morocco. Soon afterward he signaled OSS Oujda that eighty-six saboteurs were crossing the border to destroy railway lines and gasoline and ammunition dumps. Most of the eighty-six were caught.

A German spy ring was uncovered, operating around Oran. OSS agents discovered that Arab couriers were carrying documents between the Spanish Consul at Oran and the German Consul at Melilla, across the border. This came as no large surprise to the OSS. It was common knowledge that in spite of Franco's diplomatic assurances, Spain was giving every possible secret help to German and Italian subversive operations based in Spanish Morocco and directed at Allied forces in North Africa.

In discussing this problem between them, Gen. Clark and the OSS chiefs decided to attempt more extensive intelligence operations to get information from Spanish Morocco and from Spain itself. A new clandestine route was established for the infiltration of agents into Spanish Morocco and Malaga, in southern Spain. At the request of G-2 (Intelligence) Fifth Army, OSS set up a training camp for agents near Oujda, using Fifth Army equipment and funds. At this camp, on a mountaintop twenty miles from the nearest village, OSS veterans began to train thirty-five men recruited from the Spanish Republican underground—men who fought against the Franco side during the Spanish Civil War. From the Oujda camp, the trainees were sent to the OSS base at Algiers to learn secret wireless communications at the newly formed OSS radio school.

The first agents were sent to Melilla, however, without radios. A courier system was developed which appeared more reliable and more secure. Secret overland transpor-

tation was developed for agents and couriers through a
few Arab sheiks who volunteered their services. OSS
agents disguised as Arab natives were smuggled over the
border and escorted through the Spanish zone. Once
established in key positions for the observation of enemy
activity, the agents sent back biweekly reports via
couriers, who were escorted in a like manner.

Agents and couriers who took advantage of this system
had no problems. Those who tried to cross the border on
their own suffered fifty percent casualties.

In July 1943, Operation Banana was launched from
Oujda to obtain intelligence in Spain. Four trained
Spanish agents and a Spanish radio operator were
smuggled into Malaga via Tangier. Within a week, reports on Spanish defenses and other military information
were being received by OSS Oujda. Copies of these reports were sent on to Algiers and to G-2, Fifth Army. In
September, five more men entered Spain for espionage
purposes.

Unfortunately, Operation Banana was ill-conceived
and ill-executed. Actually, it should never have been
launched in the first place. For one thing, all the agents
sent from Oujda were Communists, recruited in Mexico
and North Africa through the "popular front" Union
Democratica Español. They carried, in neutral territory,
U.S. Army material, including grenades, submachine
guns, ammunition, and radios—all bearing U.S. Army
markings and registration numbers. Finally, the OSS
commander at Oujda was well aware that the territory
was already well covered by the OSS Spain unit, with
four American and more than fifty Spanish agents, who
had been filing excellent reports for several months.

The new agents from Oujda blundered, and all were caught by Spanish police, both in Melilla and Malaga. Communist codebooks were reportedly found on them, although it's possible these were planted on them by the Spanish police. But certainly they were found with their American equipment and their codebooks for communication with Oujda.

After being suitably "processed" by the Spanish police, the agents gave away the whole show. They revealed details of their training at Oujda, the use of their radios, and anything else they knew. It can be safely assumed that all this was passed on by the Spanish police to German Intelligence. The agents also gave away many of their comrades in Spain and Spanish Morocco, resulting in a roundup of 261 men by the Spanish police. Twenty-two of these men were executed.

The Spanish police complained that the United States was backing Communist revolutionaries in Spain. Since Spain was neutral territory, a country officially on friendly terms with the United States, it was a blunder to give American arms and material to agents with Communist affiliations.

The blame had to fall on the OSS commanding officer at Oujda. He had been warned that the agents recruited from the UDE would prove to be unreliable. He knew that OSS Spain was operating in the same area. It turned out that he had never cleared the Banana operation with OSS Washington, which he should have done, considering that he intended to operate in a neutral country.

Officially, the United States never admitted that the agents were sent by the OSS. Ambassador Hayes denied any knowledge of the affair. Nevertheless, the Spanish government was not impressed by the denials. Operation Banana nearly ended all OSS activity in Spain and in southern France as well.

Still, aside from Banana, the OSS proved itself in North Africa, its testing ground. Gen. Clark was well satisfied. His long supply lines were secure against sabotage. He was well informed of enemy activities on his flank and on military developments in Spain. A great many French and German agents in his zone had been caught and imprisoned. Advance agents, such as Tommy in southern France, were providing information which would prove useful to future U.S. military operations.

On September 9, 1943, on the request of Gen. Clark, an OSS detachment left Africa with him to accompany the landings at Salerno, in the invasion of Italy. Oujda was closed down, but in Tangier, Casablanca, Tunis, and Oran, the OSS remained in business until the end of the war.

LONDON:
Preparing to Storm the Continent

Although North Africa was the first active theater of operations for the OSS, a much earlier base of operations was established in London. As far back as August 1941, before the United States entered the war, Gen. Donovan began to organize an office there in liaison with the British Special Operations Executive. In November of that year, an office of the Coordinator of Information was opened, which then became the OSS office the following year. Eventually, London OSS was to be staffed by more than 2,000 men.

The British welcomed United States entry into the area of Intelligence and Special Operations. However, friction inevitably developed over divisions of command and responsibilities out of London, just as it inevitably developed among British and American field commanders.

The three most secret branches of the OSS were Secret Intelligence (SI), Special Operations (SO), and Counter-Espionage (X-2). These were established to

correspond with their British counterparts, Secret Intelligence Service (SIS), Special Operations Executive
(SOE), and Military Intelligence 6 (MI6).

Since Gen. Donovan accepted that the SO and X-2
departments were more or less special wartime organizations, he was willing to let these coordinate with SOE
and MI6, and in fact operate virtually under their control. But SI was another matter. Donovan envisioned
Secret Intelligence as a permanent organization (it later
became the nucleus of the CIA). He wanted SI to work
independently, and he fought hard for this independence.

In 1942, a series of high-level meetings began in London, with the assigned purpose of hammering out an
agreement on coordination between the two Intelligence
services. There was little argument in the area of
counterespionage and in special operations. The OSS
recognized that in the area of counterespionage the
British were—of necessity—years ahead. Therefore, OSS
would take the lead from MI6 and work under its guid-
ance.

With special operations, geographic spheres of responsibility were worked out. All operations conducted
by either OSS-SO or British SOE would be under control
of the agency to which the area was assigned. SOE was
given responsibility for France, and indeed most of
Europe, the Middle East, and West Africa. OSS-SO was
given North Africa, Finland, part of Norway, Bulgaria,
and Rumania. This did not mean that those areas designated would be the exclusive responsibility of the separate services; it did mean that when a joint operation

was launched, it was clear which service was in charge.

The SI-SIS relationship was not so easy to define. Here, too, the British wanted complete integration. They argued that this was necessary to avoid wastage of manpower, assure maximum coverage of enemy territory, and prevent accidental "blowing" of agents. They argued further that, since British Intelligence was far more experienced and already had espionage agents in the field, its organization should be in control.

This was precisely what Donovan wanted to avoid. His position was that freedom from the knowledge and control of any outside power—however friendly—was essential to long-range espionage plans. Over British opposition, OSS London was already in business with the various foreign governments-in-exile having Intelligence services in London. When OSS London began to make plans for conducting espionage on the continent of Europe, the British voiced strong objections. Donovan then took his case to the Joint Chiefs of Staff—the supreme commanders of the United States military services responsible for the conduct of the war.

Said Donovan, ". . . the British proposal suggests 'coordination' and 'agreement,' but as employed here the word 'coordination' means 'control' and 'agreement' means 'dependence.'

". . . We think it proper that in strictly physical operations we should not only be coordinated but should accept the leadership of SOE. This we do. But the attempt of the British, by reason of their physical control of territory and communication, to subordinate and control the American intelligence and counterintelligence service is short-sighted and dangerous to the ultimate interest of both countries."

Donovan won his point. The JCS gave OSS the green light to conduct espionage as it saw fit. Although SI continued to have its problems in relationships with the British in the area of espionage, it proved its value in the long run.

London was the gathering place for all the governments-in-exile, the governments of all the countries conquered by Germany whose members had fled, refusing to work with the Nazis. All these governments had Intelligence services, and all were eager to help OSS with information. But the British were extremely jealous of their own counterintelligence section and refused joint operations with everybody except X-2 of the OSS.

It seems rather strange that the British Secret Intelligence Service would create problems in the area of gathering intelligence from the enemy, and yet be so willing to cooperate in the area of counterintelligence. The OSS explanation was that since X-2 was in the position of being controlled by the British, this was perfectly satisfactory. What displeased SIS, and what created the friction, was the insistence of OSS to an independent espionage section, a section which the British knew would compete with theirs and would remain in service long after the war was over.

In any case, there was no doubt that in 1943 British counterintelligence was the most experienced and efficient in the world, and therefore its operations a closely guarded secret. Yet they took on the apprentice OSS agents willingly and helped train them. Some agents were assigned for training in the most secret of all departments, MI5, the double agent section, made famous in recent years by its illustrious fictional hero, James Bond.

The OSS agents were given complete access to MI5 files and met both double agents and controlled enemy agents. They helped to gather the "chicken feed" which was to be transmitted to the Germans by these double agents and controlled agents. The system worked like this: a double agent was an agent whom the Germans thought worked for their own intelligence service. However, he was in fact a British agent. He might have been a British agent originally, who was sent deliberately onto the Continent years earlier to infiltrate the German Intelligence system and become part of it, or he might have been a German agent originally who—for money, or change of heart, or to save his neck—became a British agent while his original masters thought he was still working for them.

This could become extremely complicated because every now and again a double agent was in fact a triple agent; he could be working for neither Germany nor the British but really for Russia. Or, he could pretend to have been bought over by the British from the Germans, but still be working for the Germans. Of course, this worked in all directions. Double and triple agents were all over Europe during the war, and this system is still active today.

A controlled agent was simply an enemy agent caught in the act and "persuaded" by one means or another to remain at his post and transmit information under control. Thus, in London, German agents who were caught were not always put in prison. A few were willing to work under control of MI5/X-2. These agents were given "chicken feed" to transmit; that is, relatively unimportant intelligence information which sounded good and which was accurate, but which could do the Allied cause little damage.

Whether an OSS agent worked in espionage, special operations, or counterespionage, he needed a variety of basics before he could go into the field. His success as an agent depended in good measure on his own ingenuity, wit, and personality. However, no matter how clever he might be, he could not expect to succeed and survive operating in enemy territory without such essentials as clothing and documents correct to the minutest detail. The agent's morale, which was of vital importance, depended to a substantial extent on the confidence he had in his "cover" identity and in the authenticity of his clothing, cigarettes, matches, identity papers, and so forth.

It is interesting to note that out of necessity, agents were sometimes sent into the field when their station chiefs knew very well that their clothing and documents were *not* in order. But the agents themselves did not know this and could not be told, because part of their cover in enemy territory was complete self-confidence. A nervous-acting agent would be gobbled up swiftly by the Gestapo.

This may sound heartless and ruthless, perhaps even immoral. But there was little room for squeamishness when the Allies were fighting for survival against an enemy almost unequalled in history for ruthlessness and cruelty. There was even less room for sensitivity in those dark areas of espionage and sabotage, where an agent was sometimes called upon to do things that even in wartime might be considered by some to be questionable. Further, an agent in enemy territory walked a very delicate tightrope; one slip could mean not only his own death, but the deaths of an entire circuit of agents.

An agent codenamed Ludovic, for example, came back from a mission into France with a complaint that his predecessor had been caught and killed and the man's circuit blown. Ludovic said that London had known this, yet had sent him in to replace the dead man without warning him of the danger.

The answer Ludovic got was that his mission had been successful, but that had he gone out knowing the fate of the other agents, he could not have acted with the confidence he actually did display, and the difficult mission could not have succeeded.

The point is arguable. Nevertheless, both OSS and the British SIS did use this reasoning in sending agents out with less than perfect cover and with less than complete information. Of course, no one has ever tried to claim that the espionage and sabotage business was anything but a rough and dirty game. The men who ran it, who were responsible for sending agents on their missions, had to be cold, calculating, and impersonal. Agents were all volunteers and they all understood the risks.

It must be said that in most cases, agents were sent on missions fully briefed and as perfectly clothed and documented as possible. With experience gained in the field—albeit the hard way—mistakes were corrected.

The clothing and documents section for OSS was in

the heart of London. There were a tailor, a cobbler, printing presses, photoengraving equipment, and experts in the field of textiles and paper. Examples and samples of uniforms, civilian clothing, and "pocket" items were stored and filed. These things had to be constantly updated for accuracy. Agents were sent regularly onto the Continent to obtain the latest changes in such items as clothing and identity papers.

No detail was too insignificant to ignore. Buttons had to be sewn on by threading the holes in parallel, Continental style, instead of in crisscross fashion. Inside jacket pockets were fitted on both sides. Sometimes a tailor's slip would be sewn on the inside of the left pocket. Suspender buttons might be marked "elegant," or "for gentlemen," or "mode de Paris," as was found to be customary on both German and French clothes.

When actual clothing could be brought back by agents, these were the items used. But there was never enough, and clothing had to be made and faked in London. The new clothing was then dirtied and cleaned several times over to give it a well-worn appearance.

Inevitably, a "sameness" crept into the type of clothing made. After a time, agents returning to London from long missions in the field reported that they could often recognize an OSS or British agent (otherwise unknown to them) by the clothing he wore and the suitcase he carried. Fortunately, the Germans never caught on to this, although eventually they did come to recognize an OSS or British-supplied wristwatch.

From the British SIS, the London OSS section learned about another detail that had to be attended to: Every agent going on a mission had to have all his American dental work redone in the French style (most agents assumed French identities on the Continent).

The preparation of false identity papers and similar documents was equally important. Every person in Europe had to carry an identity card, and movement was severely restricted for security reasons. The Gestapo constantly spot-checked for proper travel documents, work permits, and identity cards. The British told OSS that in the early days they lost many agents because SIS provided too many with identity papers from the same towns, and the Gestapo soon caught on and arrested *everybody* who claimed to be from those towns.

OSS therefore set up a special French Documents Section under a Special Operations officer. This section collected samples of occupied French papers and built up files on such items as schools, businesses, prison camps, results of bombing raids, etc., so that documents could be faked. It was a good idea, for example, to give an agent papers indicating residence and birth in a town where all official records were known to have been destroyed in an air attack. Thus the Germans would have no way of double-checking their authenticity.

Aware of this fake documentation, of course, the Germans constantly changed identity and travel papers in an attempt to trap American and British agents. It took time for the new documents to get back to London and more time to fake them accurately. Papers, inks, and type faces had to be matched perfectly for color, texture, and age. On one occasion, British SIS spent two years working on a single document to make it look authentic.

For aging, papers were sometimes rubbed in ashes or

in a powder made of crushed rock. Corners were rounded by sandpaper. Training officers also carried documents in their hip and shirt pockets for weeks until they were properly sweated.

For a time the Germans devised a new identity card for their police and Gestapo inspectors which completely baffled the London documents section. This new card had a nine-digit number, and an inspector could tell at a glance whether or not a person's card was authentic. A number of agents were picked up until experts in London broke the code of the numbering system. Here is how it worked:

Each city in France was given a number, which was represented by the first three digits of the nine-digit number. The next five digits represented the day, month, and year of the bearer's birth. The last number indicated the bearer's sex: an even number was male, an odd number, female.

Once this was known, an agent was able to steal the secret list of all the cities in France with their corresponding code numbers. The rest was easy.

Armed with proper documents, clothing, and accessories, an agent needed one more item: a cover story. He had to have an identity, a job, a reason for being where he was, doing what he was doing. Where possible, this cover story, this identity, was suited to the agent's background and personality as closely as possible.

At this time, every single refugee who had fled to Britain had a case history file with British Intelligence. From these files of real individuals, cover stories were fabricated for agents. Each story was carefully built up and drilled into the agent. As part of his training he was subjected to severely realistic interrogation by senior officers in an attempt to break down the cover story. By the time an agent was sent into the field, his cover story was as watertight as the story of his own life.

One agent, for example, was arrested because the Germans did not believe his story that he was a repatriated prisoner from a German concentration camp. When questioned by the Gestapo, he was able to give a complete detailed description of the camp, knew the names of other prisoners, the name of the camp commandant, the prison doctor, even the names of some of the guards.

A German soldier who had been a guard at the camp was called in to verify the story. The guard admitted that everything the man said was absolutely accurate. The Gestapo released the agent, after apologizing for arresting him.

When possible, an agent found a job corresponding to his actual profession. One such agent, who was in Special Operations, was sixty years old, an artist of real quality. Codenamed Aramis, this agent spent his time roaming the countryside and the streets of Paris, easel and paints in hand, untouched and unquestioned, partly because of his age.

Aramis spent a lot of time on the Left Bank of the Seine in Paris. While presumably sketching the beautiful bridges across the river, he was actually drawing a plan of all strong points fortified by the Germans along both banks. He was also used by sabotage groups as a lookout while they prepared blasting charges in strategic places.

There was one weakness in the cover story of Aramis.

He never sold a painting. Thus, if ever questioned about it, he could not have explained his source of money.

London was also the communications center for all agents operating in Europe who were outside of the Algiers network. Algiers covered the entire Mediterranean area, and its activities in southern France were aimed at gathering intelligence and committing sabotage in advance of Operation Anvil, the American invasion of southern France in August 1944. Algiers of course was linked by radio with London, which covered the rest of Europe, and which was preparing for Operation Overlord, the invasion of France across the English Channel, scheduled for June 1944.

The London communications center was made operational in September 1942, on Grosvenor Street, near the site of the present United States Embassy building. Initially, OSS used existing British communications circuits. Later, stations Charles and Victor were established to link up directly with OSS agents on the Continent. As plans for the invasion of France at Normandy were formed, station Charles was given responsibility for communications with the Special Operations teams in France and for communications with the Jedburgh teams. More about the Jedburghs later.

Communications were sent by a variety of codes and by varying sets of prearranged recognition signals. Teams in the field were assigned specific times of the day and a range of frequencies to use when transmitting; this was necessary not only for security, but to prevent a traffic jam of messages coming into London all at the same time on similar frequencies.

LONDON:
Special Operations

Special Operations/London, set up in early 1943, had as one of its primary tasks the building up of a strong and effective resistance force in France. Independent resistance groups were already in existence, but they needed help in the form of organization, arms, funds, supplies, and training. British SOE was already involved; in the autumn of 1943, SO joined the game.

Recruits for Special Operations were drawn from officers and men of the United States Army and Navy. Perfect French accents were not required, since the SO agents would be working not as espionage agents, but in uniform, with French resistance groups. It was felt by senior OSS advisors that American officers in American uniforms would carry more weight and prestige with the resistance groups than men in civilian clothes.

All SO recruits were first sent to Franklin House, the SO reception center at Ruislip, outside London. At Franklin House, while their security was being checked, they received introductory training in small arms, map reading, close combat, and general physical conditioning.

Once security clearance had been obtained, recruits were sent to the Assessment Board, where they were given a four-day course designed to test their motivation, aptitudes, general intelligence, emotional stability, leadership, confidence, discipline, and physical stamina. A student's motivation was considered to be of primary importance; many recruits wanted to be agents for unsound reasons, among these being false heroics. The failure rate was high. Some students were given noncombat assignments within OSS/London. Others were washed out completely and returned to their previous branches of the services.

If a student passed the Assessment Board's examinations, he went on for further training. First came a five-week course which included instruction in a variety of weapons, unarmed combat (judo, for example) demolitions, guerrilla warfare, wireless operation, intelligence, the use of small boats, and organizing and equipping resistance groups.

Following this course came a week at the parachute school. Within that week they made four practice jumps, three by day and one by night. This was an amazingly intensified course in jumping, when one considers that American paratroopers spent many weeks in training before they were allowed their first practice jump. But Special Operations did not have that much time to spend on jump schooling.

After jump training, the student was ready for a "finishing" school. Here the course consisted of three weeks' instruction in all aspects of an agent's work, followed by a four-day field problem. This approximated as closely as possible the conditions a Special Operations agent might encounter in enemy-held territory. It also gave instructors the chance to judge how well a student had absorbed all the things he had been taught.

Most students followed this field trial with a course at one of the specialized schools. Some became radio operators, others became experts in industrial sabotage, demolitions, weapons, street fighting, and in the use of Lysander and C-47 aircraft in the pickup and delivery of agents in hostile territory.

It is worth noting here that because of the way the radio school was operated, there could be no disastrous "play back" by the Germans of an agent in the field, as there was with Dartmouth in France and Austria. It will be remembered that the Dartmouth agent controlled by the Germans was recruited in the field, and neither Tommy nor station Algiers had either trained the agent or knew him well. No such error was made at the London Special Operations school.

Each student at the SO/London school kept the same instructor all through his course. Before a student went into the field, he actually had to operate a clandestine radio from some city in England, sending messages in code to his instructor. The instructor kept every sheet of paper used by the student during the course, because it was found that wireless operators tended to repeat the same mistakes in transmission over and over again, especially when working under pressure. Later, instructors were able to decode garbled messages from their former students in the field, because they recognized the pattern of error.

The security angle was equally important. Instructors came to know a student's "fist"—the way he sent Morse code. Thus, for example, when messages from an agent codenamed Liontamer began to come in from France after a two-week gap of silence, his instructor was called in to receive. The instructor knew at once it was not his former student sending. Obviously, the Germans had captured him and his codebooks and were sending in his name.

Since part of this recognition was due to the failure of the German operator to make Liontamer's usual mistakes, the system was then applied where each student was given a special recognition code to take into the field, such as a regular spelling error, which would alert London to the fact that he was sending under control by the Germans. The agent usually had little choice in such circumstances; it was either send and receive under German control or be shot. Confident that London would recognize his code signal, the agent would send whatever the Germans told him to send and decode for the Germans what he hoped would be useless "chicken feed."

Unfortunately, there were occasional lapses in London. Due to the pressures of overwork or because messages sometimes came in heavy with static, the "control" signal was missed. In that case the field agent became an unwitting agent for the Germans, turning over genuinely confidential information. This was just another risk in the espionage game.

Before an agent was finally sent out, he was given a final refresher course. Then he was ready for "graduation"—an assignment in enemy territory. The agent was infiltrated into France, at times by small boat across the Channel or on foot across the Swiss or Spanish border, but usually via parachute drop. Though the original plan was to send Special Operations agents into France in uniform, this was eventually modified. Before D-Day, June 6, 1944, agents were dropped in civilian clothes, with proper cover stories and documents. After D-Day, some agents and all the Jedburgh teams dropped in uniform.

There was a bit of controversy over this decision. Some senior officers thought it would be a good idea to drop uniformed officers before D-Day. This, they argued, would be a boost for French morale and would dismay any Germans who saw them or heard about them. The argument against this was that it might create an overreaction among the French, who might then start an uprising against the Germans prematurely—with disastrous results.

There was a limit to the effectiveness of the various French resistance groups. The OSS/SOE command did not want to overstep these limits; in fact, part of the Special Operations agents' task was to channel the enthusiasm of the resistance groups and coordinate them with Allied aims before and after D-Day.

Precise plans to that effect were drawn up as early as September 1943. At a series of meetings in London, a working party from SO, SOE, and the Free French (represented by Gen. P. J. Koenig) agreed that the main effort before D-Day should be directed toward sabotage of factories, power plants, and fuel shortage dumps, to decrease the flow of war materials to the Germans.

The planners hoped to do this with a minimum loss of French lives and property. Therefore, SO and SOE teams would direct their sabotage efforts at specific targets chosen by SHAEF (Supreme Headquarters, Allied Expeditionary Forces). The teams were to disable these installations without destroying them and without loss of French lives.

The agents were instructed to pressure the French workers and French managements to cooperate with the saboteurs by appealing to their patriotism. If this appeal did not work, then the agents were to use blackmail: cooperate or Allied bombers would be called in to destroy everything.

The first SO agent to be parachuted into France was a man named E. F. Floege, codenamed Alfred. Floege was a forty-five-year-old Chicago native, but he had lived in France for a long time, ran a bus company in Angers, and spoke fluent French. He was sent to organize a circuit called Sacristan, in the Le Mans-Nantes-Laval area. He was dropped near Tours and met by a man named Dubois, codenamed Hercule.

Dubois became Floege's wireless operator until Floege got an operator of his own, André Bouchardon, codenamed Narcisse. Floege set up his headquarters in the village of Mée, about twenty miles from Angers. He organized a group of saboteurs, working through two couriers, one of whom was his own son. In the autumn of 1943 the circuit received seven drops of arms and supplies and was just about ready to get down to serious work when, on December 21, Floege's son was picked up by the Gestapo.

One of the items of training all agents went through was enemy interrogation. They were told that even the toughest man would eventually break down under expert torture. But each agent was expected to hold out for two days, giving his colleagues time to flee the area. Then the agent was free to tell what he liked about his circuit.

But Floege's young son was no trained agent. He broke down quickly under Gestapo interrogation and gave away the addresses of all the men he knew on the Sacristan circuit. Forty-five men were arrested. Two days later, seven Gestapo men trapped Bouchardon in a restaurant in Mée. As one of them tried to handcuff him, he kicked the man in the groin. The man drew his pistol and shot Bouchardon in the chest. The SO agent fell to the floor, pretending to be dead. Three Gestapo men then bundled him into their car and drove away, leaving the other four to take care of the restaurant owner, who was presumably shot for harboring Bouchardon.

In the car on the way to Angers, two Gestapo men rode in the front, one in the back with the "corpse." They hadn't bothered to search Bouchardon, so he still had a revolver in his jacket pocket. He drew it out, then quickly shot the man next to him and the two in front. The car went out of control and crashed into a ditch. Bouchardon crawled out and made it to the house of friends nearby. Severely wounded, he decided to rest for a day, then find Floege.

The Gestapo found Floege first. He was working in his garden when he saw them coming for him, guns drawn, across the fields. They approached him from three sides; on the fourth side was a high wall—too high, the Gestapo thought, for his escape. But Floege managed to scramble over the wall and fled to the same house where Bouchardon was hiding.

The two agents went to Paris, where they hid out with the underground until they were passed on to other agents who smuggled them out to Spain. Bouchardon still had a bullet in his thorax. From Spain they returned to London at the end of February. On May 6, both agents were dropped again into France, to take over a circuit in a different district. We will meet Floege and Bouchardon (Alfred and Narcisse) again in the next chapter.

Another example of an early 1944 Special Operations circuit was codenamed Marksman. This operated in the areas of France called Haute-Savoie, Ain, and Jura, where Marksman helped organize and arm more than 1,000 Maquis troops in the mountains and directed their activities.

Marksman was a mixed team, comprising a British agent, Richard Heslop (Xavier), a Frenchman, J. P. Rosenthal (no codename available), and two Americans from SO, Denis Johnson (Gael) and Elizabeth Reynolds (Elizabeth). Johnson was the radio operator, Miss Reynolds the courier.

Miss Reynolds was one of fifty female agents sent into France. Of this number, fifteen were caught by the Germans and three by French police collaborating with the

Germans. Elizabeth Reynolds was one of the lucky ones. She was caught by the French and was still languishing in prison when liberated by advancing Allied troops.

The women caught by the Germans were the unlucky ones. Only three of the fifteen survived. Four were put in the ovens at Natzweiler concentration camp. Four were shot by the SS in Dachau concentration camp. One died of disease and starvation in Belsen concentration camp. Three were shot at Ravensbruck concentration camp.

From Denis Johnson, the wireless operator, we get a brief glimpse of what it was like to live and work with the Maquis in France.

"Some days we ate in the Tour d'Argent (an expensive restaurant in Paris); on others our meals consisted of a contemplation of the good meals we had had, and imagination flavored the saliva called forth by those recollections. Extremely rarely we slept in a bed. More often on a floor, and sometimes in a nice warm cowshed, or when the weather permitted, under the pines, wrapped in a parachute for lack of blankets.

"Once or twice we lived in a château, but we found it had a bad effect on our morale. More often we didn't sleep, especially during moon periods. We were perpetually on the alert, and from that point of view life was a strain, as there was not, as for the normal soldier, a possibility of repose behind the lines. We were always in the front lines, and more, for we did not know from which side an attack might come. . . . Barely a week went by in which the Maquis was not attacked. . . ."

Saboteurs on the Marksman circuit inflicted severe damage on the Germans. They disabled the Schmidt-

Roos ball bearing factory at Annecy and the power station at Ambrouay. Time and time again they cut railway lines, derailed trains, disabled locomotives and control stations, sabotaged machine shops, and blew up bridges.

The Germans were forced to divert thousands of troops hunting them down and defending strategic points. Ruthlessly, the German forces burned down villages and executed civilians in reprisal. In hit-and-run raids the Maquis countered by killing German troops in the hundreds. Although hampered by shortages of ammunition, they fought with rifles, grenades, and a few Sten guns against the heavy artillery and armor of the enemy.

Despite German efforts, Marksman almost completely crippled the railway system in their area, a factor which proved to be extremely valuable when the Germans needed to reinforce their frontline troops after D-Day. The circuit was finally disbanded in the autumn of 1944, when Allied troops cleared out the Germans.

OPERATION OVERLORD

All efforts of the combined Special Operations-Special Operations Executive circuits in France in 1943 and early 1944 were designed to support the coming invasion. The integration of the American, British, and French agents operating behind enemy lines was the final organization needed to carry out the plans of the Supreme Commanders.

Before D-Day, June 6, 1944, when Allied troops would storm ashore in Normandy, the agent circuits were to harass the enemy as much as possible. By acts of sabotage, by espionage, by lightning attacks on German troops, the agents would cause disruption of communications and supplies, injure the morale of the troops, and cause the enemy to divert thousands of men from defense positions to chasing the Maquis and their agent leaders.

The buildup of arms and agents was scheduled to culminate in an all-out attack on the Germans on D-Day by the Maquis. Troop trains and convoys were to be at-

tacked, raids made on enemy headquarters, bridges and
rail lines blown. During the German withdrawal from
France, the Maquis were to prevent enemy demolition of
installations needed by the Allies, such as power plants,
railroad terminals, and radio stations.

The sabotage efforts before D-Day were tremendously
successful. More than 100 factories producing war
materials for the Germans were put out of action.
Agents pretending to be traveling salesmen, completely
equipped with false documents, called on the managers
of a factory, requesting permission to sabotage certain
machines. If permission was not granted, they warned,
Allied bombers would be called in to destroy the entire
works.

Usually the managers agreed, since the alternative of a
bombing would not only destroy everything, it was
bound to kill and injure innocent French civilians. From
the Allied point of view, this method of sabotage meant
vital parts of important factories could be disabled with
an economy of aircraft and manpower, with precision,
and without alienating the French people.

The threat to bomb the factory was not an idle one. In
1943, when the Michelin family refused to put their own
tire factory out of commission with the help of sabotage
agents, the Royal Air Force knocked it to pieces in a
daylight raid.

French production of war materials was further sabotaged by the continuous destruction of the high-tension
lines carrying hydroelectric power from southern France
to the industrial users of the north. This operation was
combined with a successful effort to reduce French coal

stocks. Rail and canal systems carrying coal from the mines to industrial centers were sabotaged. More disruption was caused when miners in France and Belgium were induced to go on strike.

This double-edged sabotage operation forced many factories to run part-time or shut down completely for days at a time. When the hydroelectric power lines were cut, greater use was made of steam plants to produce electricity. Then, when coal supplies were cut off, no electricity was available at all.

The sabotage of rail communications was helped by the French workers and managers of the Société National des Chemins de Fer (National Society of Railroads). Guided by agents, these men repeatedly blew up rails, control towers and switches, derailed trains, and disabled locomotives. More than one thousand engines were crippled and five repair shops put out of action.

One of the most successful circuits carrying out sabotage of this nature was codenamed Stockbroker, although this circuit also suffered its share of tragedy. Stockbroker was first run by Harry Rée, a British SOE agent, codenamed Cesar. Rée had J. C. Young (Gabriel) as his wireless operator and Diana Rowden (Paulette) as courier. Rée was wounded in a fight with a German security officer in December 1943, but he escaped and was smuggled into Switzerland.

Young and Diana Rowden were less fortunate. An agent named Maugenet, sent from London to join them, was arrested by the Gestapo at a Paris railroad station. He was tortured and gave away his game. He also told the Gestapo that he had never met either Young or Miss

Rowden. With this information, and with certain papers found on Maugenet, the Germans were able to send one of their own men to meet the two Allied agents.

The German was able to convince Young and Miss Rowden of his identity with no trouble; they were expecting him, he had his codename (Benoit), and he had a letter to Young from his wife—taken of course from Maugenet. In short order the two agents were arrested. Young was executed at the Mauthausen concentration camp. Diana Rowden was one of four women agents given a fatal injection at Natzweiler concentration camp and then put into the crematorium there.

Stockbroker therefore needed new agents. In April 1944 an American SO agent was parachuted in to head the circuit. Though unidentified in OSS files, this was probably Paul Poitras (Paul), who was killed by German soldiers shortly afterward, trying to escape over a farmhouse wall.

The following month Floege and Bouchardon (Alfred and Narcisse) were dropped in to take over Stockbroker. With little arms and almost no explosives, Stockbroker nevertheless did considerable damage to railroads, convoys, power transformers, and factories. Agents used blackmail tactics to excellent advantage. They found that the Peugeot works were making tank turrets and persuaded management to sabotage the machinery rather than face an Allied bombing.

This liaison with Peugeot worked so well, that when replacement parts for the damaged machinery arrived at the plant, workers crippled them before they were unloaded from the trucks. This Peugeot plant actually produced very little to help the Germans.

The shortage of explosives forced Stockbroker to improvise. Soon Floege and Bouchardon added a new, cheap method of sabotage to their blackmail tactics. One day they stopped a train about two miles before the tunnel near Montbeliard Station. They persuaded the engineer and other trainmen to leave, got up steam, and started the train off on its own.

The train eventually crashed into another at the station, blocking the lines for days. This "Phantom train" operation became a standard sabotage procedure on the Stockbroker circuit and then spread to other areas as the word got around to other resistance leaders.

By the time the first Allied troops reached the Stockbroker area in late 1944, Floege had branched out on his own with a Maquis force of some 3,200 men, about half of them well-armed. The retreating Germans were constantly harassed by Floege's group; stragglers and small patrols were killed or captured. Hundreds of once-proud Wermacht troops gave themselves up to this Stockbroker Maquis.

In January 1944, the first completely inter-Allied mission went into action in southeastern France, to lead the Maquis there on pre-invasion and post-invasion missions. Codenamed Union, the mission was led by Pierre Fourcaud, a Frenchman. His two top aides were H. Thackthwaite, an Englishman, and Peter J. Ortiz, a U.S. Marine captain. Ortiz boldly wore his uniform; this was a morale tonic to the French, but reports of an American Marine captain around Lyons alerted the Germans to the mission.

The three officers quickly established liaison with

Maquis leaders in Lyons and the military chiefs in the areas of Vercors, Savoie, Drome, and Isère. They found confusion and discontent within the Maquis, for here, as mentioned earlier, there were different political groups jockeying for power, even as they all fought the Germans.

Union used its influence and its promises of more arms, equipment, and money to bind together these divergent groups and make them more efficient. As an immediate result, the Maquis threat to the Germans in this area grew rapidly. In turn, the Germans decided to vigorously attack the Maquis. Shortly after Union arrived, two small Maquis units were attacked by three hundred German troops. In the gun battle twenty Germans were killed, only three Maquis. The Maquis leaders later complained to the Union officers that they could have wiped out the Germans if they had had the proper arms. They wanted stronger weapons, such as mortars and heavy machine guns; they even wanted artillery pieces.

The needs of the Maquis were borne out when the determined Germans attacked again in February, this time using light tanks and three mechanized battalions of the 157th Division. The Maquis tried to hold on to their territory, with disastrous results. The Union officers reported back to London that they would need a heavily armed force of 7,000 men to hold the Vercors area. The men were available, but it was impossible to equip them to fight German armored divisions.

The Vercors is a mountainous region near Switzerland with an average altitude of 3,600 feet. The area is heavily wooded, surrounded by three rivers (Isère, Drôme, and Drac), and a natural stronghold for a resistance group. But the Maquis, lightly armed, with no military experience, was not meant for prolonged combat. Its strength lay in mobility, in hit-and-run tactics.

The experience in the Vercors proved this, but at tremendous cost. Before and after D-Day, the battles in this region were terrible and costly.

On June 28, three weeks after Operation Overlord was launched, the Justine mission was parachuted into the Vercors to help Union. Justine consisted of two American officers and thirteen enlisted men. A week later they were all joined by Eucalyptus, which came out of the Algiers headquarters. Eucalyptus was commanded by an English major, Desmond Longe. An important officer on his staff was an American, a bilingual lieutenant named A. E. Pecquet, an OSS radio operator.

At this point the Maquis numbered 2,000 men. On July 11 the French commander in the area, Col. Huet, mobilized all the remaining men in the area fit to fight, bringing the Vercors forces to 3,200. But they still lacked heavy arms. They had only rifles, submachine guns, and a few bazookas.

The Germans learned of this call-up by the French and retaliated by bombing the town of La Chapelle en Vercors for two straight days. Then, on the 14th, 85 American B-17 bombers dropped some 1,500 containers of supplies and arms on a strip near the town of Vassieux. The town's inhabitants ran out into the streets and waved to the bombers as they zoomed in over the rooftops.

Half an hour later the German Luftwaffe was back, bombing and strafing the town. All day long the Germans circled over the town, preventing the men from collecting the packages. At night 200 were collected; the rest lay where they fell.

Then the Germans moved in to destroy La Chapelle en Vercors and the Maquis. They shelled and bombed the town all the next day, and at night incendiaries were dropped, setting the houses afire. When the people ran out into the streets with their belongings, German fighters came in low and strafed them with their machine guns.

On the 18th, elements of three German divisions began to move in. The next day 21 German gliders landed at Vassieux, and some 450 crack SS troops entrenched themselves in the ruins of the town. The Maquis, led by the Special Operations officers, attacked the SS four times, killing 250. But the lack of heavy weapons doomed the resistance fighters.

The Germans continued to reinforce their men via parachute and glider, while the Maquis had nothing in reserve. The SS troops massacred more than 100 civilians at Vassieux, often killing entire families on sight. Of 120 houses in the town, only seven remained fit to live in.

By July 20, Vercors was bottled up by the enemy. For three more days the Germans bombed and shelled the plateau where the Maquis were dug in. All passes and roads were held by German troops equipped with artillery. Finally, on the 23rd, Col. Huet gave orders for the men to disperse.

In small groups they slipped away, disappearing into woods, the enemy in pursuit. Through it all, Pecquet, the

OSS radio operator, kept in touch with London, apprising them of the situation. The French who were there consider Pecquet to be one of the grand heroes of the battle of Vercors.

For eleven days the Special Operations section hid in the woods while German patrols scoured the area, shooting wildly into the brush. Those men who panicked and broke from cover were picked off like game birds by the German sharpshooters. The rest of the SO men waited, never speaking above a whisper, never moving more than a few feet at a time, existing on raw potatoes and a bit of cheese.

Finally, one of the Maquis guides slipped out and stole a truck. With this transport the survivors managed to slip through the enemy net. Several days later they reached Grenoble, just liberated by American troops. The men were in awful condition. All had lost considerable weight. Many had severe cases of dysentery. Three could not walk at all.

At Grenoble they learned that the Maquis had lost about 700 men at Vercors—a terrible price for the Maquis. It proved again that lightly armed guerrillas commit suicide when they try to fight a pitched battle with a heavily armed enemy. The Germans lost about 1,000 killed and wounded. But they had been forced to divert 22,000 troops to fight at Vercors, including parts of the 9th Panzer and the 189th and 157th Divisions.

There was yet another important tri-nation operation that worked in France after D-Day: these were the Jedburghs.

Ideally, a Jedburgh team was made up of an American, a Frenchman, and an Englishman. In most cases this ideal was achieved; sometimes, however, personnel of the right nationality were not available when a team was put together. Of 276 Jedburghs parachuted into France between June and September 1944, 83 were American, 90 English, and 103 French.

Each team consisted of two officers and a sergeant, who was the radio operator. The men wore uniforms and prepared no cover story. If captured, they were to demand prisoner-of-war treatment as a soldier in uniform.

The Jedburghs were trained in guerrilla tactics, demolition work, and leadership. Their job was to supplement the Special Operations circuits by helping to organize and arm the large numbers of new recruits to the resistance. These new recruits were expected to rise up in the thousands in response to the Allied call to arms on D-Day.

The Jedburghs were not given command of the Maquis units they met, since the Maquis were already well led by their own officers. But they were sent to advise, help plan sabotage actions, and organize attacks on the enemy when he began retreating from the invading forces.

During June and July, eight American officers and six radio operators parachuted behind enemy lines as part of nine Jedburgh teams. Most of these entered the province of Brittany, in northwestern France, together with units of the British Special Airborne Service, who also dropped in uniform. Each unit established contact with the local Maquis, set up radio contact with London, and arranged for the dropping of arms and equipment.

The Jedburgh teams armed and organized more than 20,000 men in Brittany. Under their direction, the Maquis kept railroad lines cut, derailed trains, destroyed engines and switch boxes, and generally paralyzed rail traffic throughout the Brittany Peninsula. According to captured German documents, this sabotage was so effective that when the 3rd Parachute Division moved out of Brittany shortly after D-Day, it was forced to use trucks, the rails being completely unreliable.

The roads were not safe either. Maquis groups led by Jedburghs constantly attacked German convoys from ambush. In Brittany the Jedburghs and the Maquis did not make the mistake that met with such disastrous results at Vercors. They did not stand and fight. On June 12, when a German infantry brigade attacked, they faded away after a brief fire fight. A week later, attacked again by an armored column, a large group of Maquis held the Germans at bay until a squadron of P-47 Thunderbolts could be called in by the Jedburgh radio operator.

When the planes attacked, the Maquis drifted away, leaving the Germans to battle thin air. This hit-and-run tactic in Brittany had a powerful demoralizing effect on the Germans, many of whom by now accepted defeat by the Allies as inevitable. It helped pave the way for the surrender of large groups of the enemy in the weeks and months to come.

During August and September, sixty-nine more American Jedburghs parachuted into France. They, too, concentrated on the sabotage of railways, roads and bridges, electric power stations, and telephone lines. The Paris-Beauvais-Dieppe railroad was cut ten times during the last two weeks in July. From June onward, the Paris-Orleans-Limoges line was completely unusable.

Jedburgh teams organized ambushes, attacks on German garrisons and convoys, and small-scale actions to mop up bypassed or isolated enemy units. On the 29th of July, for example, a Jedburgh team and seventy Maquis attacked a German column of twenty-six vehicles. They damaged six armored cars and two artillery pieces and killed twenty-nine Germans, losing just one man.

On August 2 a Jedburgh team with thirty Maquis held a road junction on the main Paris-Brest road for two days, fighting off a German antiaircraft battalion. Escaping with only two casualties, the group delayed the German retreat long enough for an American armored troop to come up and capture the Germans the next day.

Soon after D-Day the Jedburgh teams were given orders to exercise careful control over sabotage operations. They began, in effect, a *counter-scorch* policy. It was realized by Allied commanders that the retreating Germans would try to destroy everything useful behind them. The Jedburghs were instructed to limit their own sabotage operations to minor damage, just enough to prevent German use of an installation, but not so severe as to make it irreparable for Allied use.

At the same time they were to prevent German destruction of bridges, power plants, and so forth. One example of a Jedburgh success in this area occurred on August 17, when they attacked a group of Germans holding a power plant in Aveyron. Having surrounded the Germans, the Jedburgh-led Maquis held off their attack and induced the Germans to surrender. The plant was taken intact.

Typical of the Jedburghs was a team codenamed Horace (all Jedburgh teams had male first names as codenames). Horace consisted of an American officer, a French officer, and an American radio operator. They were dropped in the area of Brittany called Finistère, near the port of Brest. Their mission was to contact two Jedburgh teams and British SAS teams already in the area and to assist in organizing resistance forces around the port.

The main purpose of the mission was to divert German forces in that area from attacking the flank of American troops advancing inland from the invasion beaches. Their secondary mission was to tie down and prevent the escape of Germans trapped in pockets, until they could be rounded up by the Allied armies.

As planned, team Horace was parachuted into a field some forty miles southeast of Brest. Moving by night, hiding by day, they made arrangements for safe houses, guides, and contacts, aided by the local Maquis. Quickly they established radio contact with London. News of their arrival spread rapidly, and soon the Germans knew they were in the area. A reward of one million francs (about $25,000 then) was offered for information leading to their capture, dead or alive.

The Maquis warned the members of Horace that German repression was strong in the Brest area. Nevertheless, the three men decided to go there when all efforts to contact Jedburgh team Giles and other Maquis groups failed.

German restrictions were indeed tight. Every town and village had a German patrol or garrison. Defenses were extensive. Traffic was carefully regulated. All bi-

cycles were confiscated. Only a few Frenchmen were allowed to drive any vehicle at all—doctors with special
passes, for example, and civilian drivers of German supply trucks. There was a strict curfew. Any civilian found
on the streets after the curfew was liable to be shot on
the spot.

Team Horace persevered, however. With the aid of
two Maquis, the three men were hidden in empty wine
barrels. Then, as part of a truckload of wine for the Germans, they were driven to a wood five miles from Brest.
They spent the night in a foxhole, then proceeded the
next day, still hidden in the barrels, to a safe house near
Lesneven. The driver was stopped many times by German patrols. Fortunately, no one looked inside the barrels. At one point, when the truck developed a flat tire, a
German patrol helped the driver change it.

In the woods just outside Brest, team Horace set up its
headquarters and its radio contact with station Victor in
London. A group of Maquis couriers was recruited to pass
messages by word of mouth to other resistance fighters in
the area. In this way groups were formed to prepare
dropping grounds for supplies and for Allied personnel.

In Brest itself there was no organized Maquis. The
Gestapo had killed or captured them all. Resistance inside the city consisted of a few scattered former leaders
driven underground and a few thousand unarmed citizens who could be counted on to help. Many of these
people worked for the Germans in the dock areas. Because they carried special passes, they were able to
smuggle in small arms without being searched.

To provide arms and ammunition for others, team

Horace set up several small dumps in the countryside; each dump was known to no more than ten or twelve men. Containers and large weapons were transported from the dropping grounds under hay in horsecarts or in civilian trucks carrying supplies to the Germans. By the time the Americans attacked Brest, some 1,500 partisans had been armed.

In the meantime, team Horace provided valuable intelligence. On July 29, a French dock worker reported that the Germans planned to sink two 14,000-ton tankers in the harbor to deny its use to Allied ships. Horace radioed this information to London. Soon afterward American bombers flew over and completely destroyed these two ships. Blown to pieces, they could provide no blockage of the port.

On August 2, Horace received instructions to complete resistance plans, to get ready for the all-out attack by Allied troops on German pockets in Brittany. Resistance leaders were told to bring back information on enemy troop movements, defenses, headquarters, and so forth. Top priority was given to the preservation of bridges and tunnels and the railway lines so that Allied troops could use them.

When the first American troops appeared, on August 7, team Horace was assigned formally to G-2 (Intelligence) of the U.S. Sixth Armored Division. The team was able to turn over to divisional intelligence a suitcase full of maps and reports on coastal defenses at Brest. But intelligence officers needed more. They wanted information on the German combat defenses the division would have to face fighting its way into the city.

Thirty Frenchmen were chosen to bring out this information. In Brest, they scribbled reports and drew sketches of street barricades, antitank road blocks, and artillery observer points. Then they sneaked out of the city and reported back to the division. During the attack on Brest, which resulted in bitter house-to-house fighting, these French acted as guides and couriers, working with tremendous courage under fire.

In coordination with the main attack on Brest, Maquis forces, led by Jedburghs, ambushed enemy columns, attacked patrols, and actually freed many small villages. In one action, a small force of Maquis and Jedburghs acted as a screen between the enemy and American infantry, harassing the Germans so severely that they never realized that their force of 30,000 was facing only two American battalions.

North of Brest, Jedburgh-led Maquis surrounded a German coastal position at St. Pabu. The German commander threatened to slaughter French civilians if the resistance group did not withdraw. This information was sent back to G-2 at Sixth Armored Division. The commanding officer sent word back to the German commander that unless he surrendered, 2,500 German prisoners would be turned over to the French resistance forces.

The Germans surrendered. Two members of Horace were sent in to receive the surrender and interrogate the German commander.

This job done, Horace began working with the Second Ranger Battalion, cutting off German forces west of Brest and capturing the Conquet area. Here the Germans had heavy coastal guns and heavily mined, concrete emplacements. With Horace members acting as front line combat guides, a combined force of 600 Rangers and Maquis attacked. On September 9 the battle ended with the capture of the position, the silencing of the big guns, and the capture of 1,250 Germans. The following week, its job done, team Horace was flown back to England.

Other Jedburgh teams operating in France were equally successful. Casualties were relatively light—twenty-one were killed, none was captured.

The work of the OSS before and after Operation Overlord was officially commended by Gen. Eisenhower, Supreme Commander of the Allied Forces. In a letter to the London Chief of Station, Gen. Eisenhower said, in part, ". . . In no previous war, and in no other theater during this war, have resistance forces been so closely harnessed to the main military effort.

". . . I consider that the disruption of enemy rail communications, the harassing of German road moves and the continual and increasing strain placed on the German war economy and internal security services throughout Europe . . . played a very considerable part in our complete and final victory. . . .

"Finally, I must express my great admiration for the brave and often spectacular exploits of the agents and special groups under control of Special Force Headquarters. . . ."

OPERATION SUNRISE

The most successful OSS agency in World War II was run by Allen W. Dulles out of Bern, Switzerland. Dulles, who became a Director of the CIA after the war, hardly looked the part of a master spy, which is perhaps one reason why he was so successful. Almost fifty years old when he was hired by Donovan, Dulles was a tall, scholarly-looking man. He smoked a pipe, wore glasses, and favored tweed suits. He looked every inch the Princeton Phi Beta Kappa he was. He had taught English in a missionary school in India; he had served with the Foreign Office of the State Department in Bern and Vienna during World War I; and he had later practiced law in the office of his older brother, John Foster Dulles, destined to become Secretary of State under President Eisenhower.

Donovan wanted Dulles to head the London office of the OSS, but Dulles felt that his experience and his contacts—many of his law firm's clients had been German—would make him more valuable in Switzerland. In No-

vember 1942, therefore, he made his way to Bern via
Lisbon, Spain, and southern France. He crossed the
Franco-Swiss border by train just as the Germans moved
into southern France and sealed off the border. But for
the help of a friendly French border guard, Dulles
would have been picked up by the Gestapo then and
there and his brief career as an OSS agent terminated.

Arriving in Bern, Dulles took up his cover post as Special Assistant to the American Minister, Leland Harrison.
His real job was the coordination of espionage and sabotage missions for large areas of France, the Balkans,
northern Italy, and Germany itself.

Dulles had to play his game like a man walking on
eggs. For one thing, his arrival in Bern was duly noted
by German counterintelligence agents, and he was at
once suspect. The Germans were well aware that every
diplomatic mission everywhere in the world was used as
a cover base for intelligence activities (this is as true
now as it was then). Both the *Abwehr* (Military Intelligence) and the *Sicherheitsdienst-Ausland* (SS Secret
Service abroad) had men in Bern. They knew the OSS
was operating in Switzerland; while they could not pinpoint Dulles's specific assignment, they had good reason
to believe that he was part of the American intelligence
apparatus.

At the same time, Dulles had to respect Swiss neutrality. The Swiss had no love for the Nazis, but were
determined to maintain their position as neutrals in a
world at war. The Swiss authorities knew that if they
allowed Allied intelligence agents to operate in Switzerland too freely, Hitler might use this as an excuse to at-

tack. By maintaining an even hand with belligerents on both sides, Switzerland (like Sweden and Portugal) became a kind of neutral oasis for the intelligence services of both sides all through the war.

To keep this balance, Swiss Intelligence assigned separate sets of officers to work with each side. Col. Roger Masson was the Swiss contact man with SS General Walter Schellenberg, head of the German Secret Service. Capt. Max Waibel liaised with Dulles. These contacts were arranged so that the Swiss could keep the belligerents apart and watchdog them so that Swiss neutrality was observed.

In any case there was little danger of violence on Swiss soil. The Germans would no more have considered assassinating Dulles than Dulles would have ordered the elimination of his opposite number on the other side of town. It just wasn't done then, any more than it is now—at least on that high a level. However, a spy or saboteur caught in a combat zone was an agent of another color. Most who were caught were shot. Some unfortunate enough to fall into the hands of ruthless Nazi counterintelligence men or the Gestapo were tortured first for information.

Renting a house in Herrengasse, a picturesque street in Bern's old quarter, Dulles began to set up his base of operations. Around him he gathered a small group of aides; some were businessmen, some American diplomatic personnel, some refugees from the Nazis seeking sanctuary in Switzerland. Dulles's genius for intrigue evidenced itself early in the game when the Swiss immigration authorities moved to deport a couple of these refugee aides of his on the grounds they had "no visible means of support." Unable to admit they worked for Dulles, the refugees were at wits' end until Dulles came up with a bright idea. He got a sympathetic doctor to certify them insane and had them committed to an asylum outside Bern. There they remained throughout the war, slipping in and out of the asylum as they were needed.

For his right-hand man Dulles picked Gero von Schulze Gaevernitz, German by birth but a naturalized American. Gaevernitz had extensive business interests in Switzerland and important contacts inside Germany. His father had been a member of the German government in the pre-Hitler years. When America entered the war Gero Gaevernitz was in Switzerland on business. Reading in a newspaper about the arrival of Dulles in Bern, Gaevernitz hurried to see him. The two men had been friends for years. Trusting him implicitly, Dulles took him into his confidence and enlisted his help.

One of Dulles's early problems was communications. OSS agents in France, Italy, and Germany found ways of getting to Bern with information; the difficulty was in transmitting this information to where it could best be used—to London, Washington, or to American forces advancing in Africa. Within Switzerland itself a courier service was set up among the various OSS substations, such as Geneva, Zurich, Lugano, and Basel. But communications to the outside world was a touchy business.

Dulles had a scrambler device on his telephone; however, he knew the Swiss, and perhaps even the Germans, could unscramble him. Thus no secret information could be given over the phone. Almost every day Dulles spoke to OSS headquarters in Washington via transatlantic telephone, but the messages had to be very general in nature, limited to political and economic information.

While Switzerland was cut off, an island in a sea of German-occupied territory, Dulles did try now and then to slip a courier through the lines, hoping he would get through to London or to the OSS base in Algiers. Most of these couriers were picked up and never heard from again. There remained just one method of communication open to Dulles for the first six months or so of his mission in Bern. This was commercial radio, provided by the Swiss. Since the Germans could listen in, all messages had to be in code.

This was slow work, since Dulles had only two code clerks. Soon, however, relief came from an unexpected quarter. As American airmen began making forced landings in Switzerland, Dulles got permission from the Swiss to attach some of these men officially to his Legation staff. In short order, former pilots, bombardiers, and navigators became code clerks, working shifts around the clock.

In October 1943, when the island of Corsica was liberated from the Germans, Dulles was able to set up his first reliable courier service. It was complicated, but it worked. In Bern, reports, maps, and drawings were put on microfilm and sent to Geneva, where they were given to a locomotive engineer on the run from Geneva to Lyons in France. The film was hidden in a secret compartment built over the firebox.

From time to time the Germans stopped the train and searched it. When this happened, the engineer triggered a trapdoor which sent the film into the flames. Then, when the train returned to Geneva, he notified OSS, which made up a new set of films. At Lyons, the engineer would turn the film over to another courier, who took it to Marseilles on his bicycle. There he gave it to the captain of a fishing boat, who brought it to Corsica. A plane from OSS Algiers picked it up on Corsica. The time involved from Bern to Algiers was ten to twelve days.

As early as December 1942, one month after his arrival in Bern, Dulles began to set up an organized liaison operation with Italian partisans in northern Italy. A great many Italians were anti-Fascist and anti-Nazi, and, in the industrial north and in the Italian alpine area, bands of partisans fought a running battle with the Germans. They needed arms, ammunition, supplies, and money. Dulles meant to see that they got them.

He found an Italian-speaking American resident in Lugano. Separating Italy from Switzerland at that point was Lake Lugano. Getting across the lake, avoiding German patrol boats, was not much of a problem for anyone who knew the area well. Dulles recruited this American as his contact man with the partisans. This agent in turn made contact with an OSS partisan leader codenamed Como. Together they harassed the Germans unmercifully, blowing up trains and bridges, attacking convoys, and supplying Dulles with invaluable information about German troop movements.

When the Swiss found out about the Lugano agent they tried to put him out of business. His movements across the border, smuggling arms and ammunition, could have embarrassed them with the Germans. They tried to deport him. But Dulles persuaded the U.S. State

Department to establish an official Legation at Lugano
and to appoint his agent a Vice Consul. Now the agent
could operate (as Dulles did) under diplomatic cover,
and the Swiss could in conscience turn a blind eye to the
man's activities.

Eventually, however, the agent went too far. One day
he connived with Como to smuggle a huge cache of arms
and ammunition across the border. Como managed to
hijack a freight train. He loaded it with Swiss arms and
supplies and drove it back to the border. When the Swiss
border guards tried to stop him, he crashed the train
through the barriers and on into Italy.

The Swiss at once canceled the Lugano agent's cre-
dentials and ordered him confined to the area. Dulles
had Como switched to another area of operations to keep
the Swiss happy. But this did nothing to stop the OSS
operations in northern Italy. In fact, it was the success of
OSS activities in this area that set the stage for Operation
Sunrise, perhaps the most amazing coup engineered by
the OSS—and Dulles—in the entire war. More about
Operation Sunrise later in this chapter.

Meanwhile, Dulles expanded his operations. Early in
1943, he made two important contacts which opened up
France to OSS intelligence. The first was with the
Deuxième Bureau, operating out of the French Embassy
in Bern. The Deuxième Bureau was the very efficient
French Secret Service. When France fell and then was
fully occupied by the Germans, the Deuxième Bureau in
Switzerland was stranded without funds and without a
country. Dulles stepped in, got them money from OSS
London, and enlisted their aid. The French accepted
and turned over their network of agents in France and

Germany to Dulles. To give these Frenchmen the feeling that they were helping their own government as well, Dulles had copies of their reports sent via radio to the Free French Headquarters in Algiers.

Another important source of information on France came via an old business acquaintance of Dulles's. In March 1943, a French lawyer slipped across the border into Geneva. He got word to Dulles that he represented a strong segment of the French resistance. Dulles went to Geneva, met with him in secret, and began the nucleus of a French resistance cell in Geneva which would operate in conjunction with the OSS bureau there. Soon afterward, the commander of the largest Maquis group in France, which operated in the Savoy region, met Dulles in Geneva and gave him details of his operation. He also asked Dulles for money and supplies, which Dulles got him via London.

From these French sources, operating a regular courier service across the border into Geneva, Dulles was able to supply a wealth of information to London. He reported on troop movements, submarine bases, resistance activities, and general conditions in France and Germany.

The importance of the Bern mission in its support of partisan activities in France and northern Italy cannot be overstated. The same applies to the value of intelligence information received through these channels. However, these pale in the light of Dulles's incredible contacts with the Germans themselves.

Dulles's friend Gero Gaevernitz was convinced that there were many more Germans who were anti-Nazi

than was generally believed among the Allies. Dulles
was inclined to agree with him, based on his own knowledge of Germany. Both felt that among these anti-Nazis
were people of importance in industry and government.
If contact could be made, important results might be obtained.

Accordingly, Dulles did not go too far underground,
as espionage phraseology would put it. He wanted to
remain available to any Germans looking for an American agent to contact. Obviously, any highly placed German who wanted to help the Allied cause would go
about this very carefully indeed. He would not take the
chance of a "small-time" contact with a field agent. He
would want to go directly to a high-ranking intelligence
officer, such as Dulles. And he would need first to make
this contact via a friendly and trusted intermediary. This
is where Gaevernitz proved to be invaluable.

One evening early in 1943, Gaevernitz sneaked into
Dulles's house through the rear entrance via a protected
vineyard. With him he had Hans Bernd Gisevius, Vice
Consul in the German Consulate General in Zurich.
Gisevius was also an officer in the *Abwehr* and anti-Hit-
ler. Recently returned from Berlin, Gisevius reported
that there was a plot cooking among a number of German generals to get rid of Hitler. He was part of the
conspiracy, and he wanted to cooperate with American
intelligence.

To prove his good faith, he drew from his pocket the
texts of several secret telegrams which had been sent to
Washington by the American Legation in Bern. The
Gestapo had broken the State Department code, which,

because OSS was so understaffed, had been used occasionally for long reports of a political nature. Among these secret reports was one mentioning that Count Ciano, the Italian Foreign Minister, was interested in overthrowing Mussolini, the Fascist dictator, and joining the Allies.

The Gestapo showed the cable to Hitler, who showed it to Mussolini. Count Ciano was promptly executed.

Dulles passed the news of the broken code on to the American Minister. The code was changed, but gradually. Had it been changed immediately the Germans would have been tipped off that OSS Bern knew the code had been broken. Suspicion would have been aroused that someone in the Swiss-based *Abwehr* had "gone over"—that is, turned enemy agent.

Having shown his good faith and that he could produce high-level intelligence material, Gisevius began a long, fruitful association with Dulles. He helped the OSS penetrate the German Legation and the various German Consulates in Switzerland. Very little went on in German diplomatic circles or among the *Abwehr* sections that OSS didn't know about.

As time went on, Gisevius revealed to Dulles the names of all the conspirators in the plot to kill Hitler. Dulles gave the codename Breakers to this plot. It took eighteen months to hatch. During this period, Gisevius told Dulles that the conspirators were most anxious to enlist active American support. Dulles forwarded the suggestion to Washington. Both Donovan and President Roosevelt gave an emphatic "no" to OSS cooperation with the plotters.

The assassination attempt of Hitler, which took place on July 20, 1944, was a failure. Most of the conspirators were executed. Gisevius hid in Berlin for six months, escaping the Gestapo dragnet. He got word to Dulles of his whereabouts. To help protect him, Dulles leaked the rumor that Gisevius had escaped to Switzerland. The Gestapo combed the country for him. Eventually, when the search cooled down, OSS obtained a complete set of new Gestapo identity papers for Gisevius. In January 1945, he did cross the border into Switzerland, and thus survived.

After the war, much was written about this refusal of OSS to help kill Hitler. It was pointed out that with OSS help, the plot might well have succeeded, or an alternate plan contrived which might have done away with Hitler. With Hitler gone, the new leaders would have brought the war to a quick end in 1944. Thousands of lives could have been saved. The entire course of history altered.

This of course is hindsight. And it is impossible to say what course history might have taken had the conspirators killed Hitler in July 1944. At the time, those in power, who had to make that kind of decision, had good reason to stay clear of assassination attempts against any country's leader, no matter how terrible he might be.

For one thing, it was against American principles to assassinate a head of state. America, and the OSS, was not in the business of political assassination. If the United States was seen to approve of its own agents engaging in political assassination, then ten years later, or twenty years later, or a century later, it could have no cause to complain if agents of other countries did the same to the heads of state of countries they considered to be enemies and its leaders evil.

But aside from the moral arguments against OSS involvement in the killing of Hitler, there was a more practical political consideration. Hitler, in his rise to power, constantly trumpeted to the German people that the German Army had never been actually defeated in World War I. He blamed the loss of that war on traitors and conspirators in the German government.

It was because of the power of that myth, still held in Germany by many people in 1944, that the Allies had established the principle of "unconditional surrender." There would be no deals, no Armistice. The German Army and the German leaders would have to publicly admit they had been beaten and surrender.

Therefore, had the OSS helped to kill Hitler before the German Army had been thoroughly defeated in the field, there would have remained the very real possibility that one day a new Hitler would emerge in Germany who could once more try to rally the German people with the argument that traitors and plotters had defeated Germany, not the Allies. Such a demagogue could further point an accusing finger at OSS assassins.

Considering the world situation today it is possible to take various views on whether or not killing Hitler in 1944 was worth the possible consequences. It's a moot question. One can only say that in 1944, the high-level decision to keep the OSS out of any assassination plots against Hitler was based on what appeared to be prudent then and there.

Gisevius was not the only, or the most important, of

Dulles's German contacts. Among the others were Otto Kiep, an officer in the Foreign Ministry (caught by the Gestapo and executed in 1944), Hans Berndt von Haeften, Adam von Trott du Solz (executed by the Gestapo in August 1944, for his part in the plot against Hitler), and Dr. William Hoegner.

Through these and other sources, Dulles got from Germany detailed information on military plans and industrial production. Among other items, OSS Bern reported on the new midget "Beetle" tank a full year before it made its first battleground appearance at Anzio, Italy.

OSS Bern was first to report on new secret weapons being developed, including the V-1 and V-2 rockets. The first reports on the rockets got to Dulles as early as February 1943. An industrialist told him a new kind of aerial torpedo was being developed. Then, in May, Gisevius told him that the Germans had developed a new heavy missile using the rocket principle. It was already in production. In June, Dulles was able to pinpoint the assembly plant and testing ground: Peenemunde.

On August 16, 1943, RAF bombers raided Peenemunde, badly damaging the installation and setting back the V-rocket program by many months (the "V" in the designation came from the German word, *Vergeltungswaffen*, meaning reprisal weapon). The implications of this setback to the German rocket program were enormous and only later appreciated. Hitler had hoped to have rockets over England by the end of November 1943. This was Program A-4, so designated by Hitler himself.

These powerful V-1 and V-2 rockets, launched on schedule at the end of 1943, could have devastated English cities. Perhaps more important, these rockets could have wrecked the buildup of Allied invasion forces along the English coast in May 1944, and even destroyed the D-Day invasion fleet on June 6. But, due to the information collected by Dulles and the subsequent RAF raid, the V-rocket program was delayed until June 1944. By then its effectiveness was limited. Furthermore, OSS Bern had discovered many of the launching sites along the French coast. Armed with these specific targets, the RAF and the American Eighth Air Force bombed and destroyed seventy-three of the ninety-six launching sites known to have existed.

The most valuable German contact of them all, a man rated by both OSS and the British Secret Service as the best single intelligence source of the war, was a man whose codename was George Wood. His real name has never been revealed.

George Wood was an older man, described by Dulles as short and balding. He had served with the German Foreign Office in Berlin for many years, before Hitler came to power. He was bitterly anti-Nazi. In 1943, he was sent often as a courier to Switzerland, and it was then, on August 23, 1943, that he made contact with Dulles.

He came secretly to the house on Herrengasse late that night. With him he carried a bulky brown envelope, the Nazi swastika stamped on red sealing wax.

Opening the envelope, he said to Dulles, "You will find here 186 separate items of information."

Dulles could hardly believe his eyes. The papers spread before him were stamped *Geheime Reiche Sache* —Secret State Document. They included cables and dispatches between the Foreign Office in Berlin and German diplomatic posts all over the world.

Carefully, Wood revealed that while he was a loyal German, he hated the Nazis and knew they would destroy his country. For some time, he explained, he had sent bits and pieces of information to the French and British through a contact he had in the French resistance. But when he knew he was being sent to Bern as an official courier, he decided to make contact with American intelligence. He had a close friend in Bern, a German who was already in contact with Dulles, and thus the meeting with Dulles had been arranged.

For the purpose of OSS intelligence, his job in Berlin was uniquely useful. He handled all the cable traffic through the Foreign Office. He was able to make copies of those documents he could not physically take out of Berlin, and since he was expected to make frequent courier visits to Switzerland, he would be able to feed Dulles regularly.

Over the next several months George Wood brought to Dulles a treasure trove of information: submarine routings, Luftwaffe losses and strength, the effects of Allied bombings of Germany, military plans, technical information on new weapons.

Among his more remarkable revelations to Dulles was the fact that the Germans had a spy in the British Embassy at Ankara, Turkey. He showed Dulles a copy of a cable from Franz von Papen, the German Ambassador in Turkey, to Berlin, boasting about top secret documents he had been obtaining from this agent.

This agent was the famous "Cicero," an Albanian valet of the British Ambassador. Cicero, whose real name was

Elyesa Bazna, was not motivated by any love for Germany or hatred for the Allies. He was an ordinary man who had long dreamed of amassing a fortune—illegally if possible. Cicero spied for money.

Obtaining a duplicate set of keys to the Ambassador's safe, he opened it whenever he was alone in the house and filmed top secret documents. He turned over to his German contact in Ankara. L. C. Moyzisch, such items as the names of British agents in Turkey, details of the Casablanca conferences attended by Roosevelt, Churchill, and Stalin, and preliminary plans for the Allied invasion of Europe.

When George Wood informed Dulles of Cicero's activities, Dulles at once passed the information to his British colleagues in Bern. Shortly afterward, in the guise of a "routine visit," security inspectors turned up at the British Embassy in Ankara and changed the locks on the safe. The British had to make the change look routine and could not arrest Cicero, lest they tip off the Germans that there was a major leak somewhere within their own security system.

Cicero eventually quit, with well over a million dollars in British currency hidden away—the highest-paid spy of the war. However, the irony of the story is that when he was finally apprehended—when it was safe to do so—it was discovered that all his money was counterfeit. The Germans had been doublecrossing him all along. His "fortune" was useless.

Toward the end of 1944, to make the transmission of documents easier, OSS supplied Wood with a miniature camera. Wood then began to photograph documents and

send Dulles rolls of film. He sent this film in envelopes
addressed to an imaginary girl friend in Switzerland and
used German couriers who had no idea of what they
were carrying. Wood, with the connivance of a doctor
friend, would remove secret documents from his office in
Berlin and photograph them in the basement operating
room of a hospital.

Once, during a filming period, Wood learned that
Himmler, the head of the dreaded SS, was in his office
looking for a particular file—a file then in the process of
being filmed. Wood rushed back to his office and pre-
tended to pull from a filing cabinet the file he was actually taking out of his coat pocket.

Out of all this intrigue, from all these valuable contacts
with cooperative Germans, came Allen Dulles's most sen-
sational coup of the war. The OSS codenamed it Operation Sunrise.

In November 1944, OSS teams in northern Italy reported "feelers" from German sources, indicating a desire to surrender. But in the follow-up to these "feelers,"
the Germans involved invariably insisted on certain conditions. These conditions were always refused. Allied
terms continued to be unconditional surrender.

Then, on Sunday, the 25th of February, 1945, Max
Waibel, now a Major in Swiss Military Intelligence, contacted Dulles and Gero Gaevernitz and asked for a meeting. The three men had dinner together in a restaurant
on Lake Lucerne. Waibel told Dulles that he had
another peace feeler—but this one looked genuine. The
approach had come via an Italian industrialist, Baron
Luigi Parilli, and a Swiss, Professor Max Husmann. They

were now in Lucerne, ready to talk to the OSS, with an offer from SS *Obergruppenfuhrer* (General) Karl Wolff to surrender all German and Italian Fascist forces in northern Italy.

Dulles was cautious. It might be another false alarm. Worse yet, it might be an attempt by German agents to penetrate the OSS in Switzerland. He therefore returned to Bern, but sent Gaevernitz to meet Parilli and Husmann.

As a result of this meeting, Gaevernitz reported to Dulles that Parilli and Husmann had been in direct contact with two SS officers from Milan—Capt. Guido Zimmer and his immediate superior, Col. Eugen Dollman. Both these officers, though members of the SS, were appalled at Nazi plans to destroy all of northern Italy as the Allies advanced; these plans included the destruction of invaluable art treasures in addition to industry.

According to Zimmer and Dollman, General Wolff felt the same way, and he was willing to surrender to prevent the orders from Berlin being carried out.

Although this sounded promising to Dulles, he was not yet convinced that the two men were telling the truth; or, if indeed they were, that the SS officers involved could pull off the surrender.

For the moment, Dulles put the notes of this first meeting in his already bulging file called "Peace Feelers." He didn't think it would really come to much.

But then, five days later, an urgent message came from Maj. Waibel: Capt. Zimmer and Col. Dollman were in Switzerland, in a hotel in Lugano. They wanted to meet with the OSS chief.

Dulles was still not ready. He knew the value of holding back. He, the mission chief, should meet only with the top man on the other side, not two messengers. Accordingly, he sent one of his agents, Paul Blum, to meet with Capt. Zimmer and Col. Dollman.

Blum had orders from Dulles. He transmitted them to the two SS officers: If they were serious, and if they had the power and the backing of Gen. Wolff, then they would have to prove it. Blum handed Col. Dollman a slip of paper upon which were written two names, Ferruccio Parri and Antonio Usmiani. Parri was one of the leaders of the Italian resistance; Usmiani was an Italian who worked as an agent for the OSS in Italy. Both men had been caught by the SS and were in prison, Parri in Verona, Usmiani in Turin.

Dulles wanted both men released and brought to him in Switzerland. If Gen. Wolff could do this then he would prove both his good intentions and his power in Italy.

Col. Dollman was obviously shaken by this request. Parri in particular was the most valuable prisoner the SS held. But he would talk to Wolff and he would see what could be done. He and Zimmer then left Lugano and returned to Milan.

Dulles thought then that he would hear no more from the Germans. He knew he had given Wolff a very difficult test. But he felt that if Wolff could not or would not release the two men, then he would not or could not bring in the surrender of all enemy forces in northern Italy.

On March 8, Maj. Waibel telephoned Dulles with the news: Parri (later to become Prime Minister of

Italy) and Usmiani were safe in Switzerland. What was more, and perhaps equally startling, Gen. Wolff, along with Col. Dollman, Capt. Zimmer, and a Maj. Wenner, had crossed the border and were on a train bound for Zurich.

Dulles appreciated the risk Wolff and the others had taken. It was a five-hour train ride from the border town of Chiasso to Zurich. Wolff's photo had often been in the Swiss newspapers. Should he be recognized by any German agent along the way, he was as good as dead on his return to Italy.

But Maj. Waibel had helped with the security precautions. The group traveled in two separate compartments on the train, with doors locked and curtains drawn. Should any passenger be curious, Waibel had arranged a cover story that these were German businessmen (they wore civilian clothes) on their way to Zurich for a conference with the Swiss.

Dulles jumped in his car and drove to Zurich. Gero Gaevernitz took the train from Davos, where he'd been skiing. Now Dulles was ready to meet with Gen. Wolff. He was impressed with the SS Commander's confidence in leaving his post in Italy to meet in Switzerland and with his swift release of the two prominent Italian prisoners. But first, to satisfy himself that it was indeed Parri and Usmiani being held as "patients" in a Zurich clinic, Dulles and Gaevernitz went to meet the two men.

It was indeed Parri and Usmiani. The two men were bewildered at the sudden turn of events. When the SS came to their cells and took them out, they assumed they were being led away to be shot. Now they were safe in

Switzerland. Each had the same question for Dulles, whom they knew, of course: "What was going on?"

Dulles could not tell them, but he assured them that it was best they remain in hiding in Zurich for the time being.

From the clinic Dulles went to a secret apartment he kept in Zurich. There he awaited the arrival of the German officers. Also at the meeting were Gaevernitz, Parilli, and Husmann.

Speaking directly to Dulles, Wolff said that he admitted being a follower of Hitler. But in the past year he had come to realize that the war was lost, and that to continue was a crime against the German people. He felt, as a good German, that it was his duty to bring the war to an end as soon as possible.

He understood and accepted that the only Allied terms were unconditional surrender. "I control the SS forces in Italy," he told Dulles. "And I am willing to place myself and my entire organization at the disposal of the Allies to terminate hostilities."

Dulles replied that while this was encouraging, Gen. Wolff himself had a superior: Field Marshal Albert Kesselring. What were his feelings?

Wolff replied that he was on good terms with Kesselring. He had discussed with him surrendering to the Allies. Kesselring had not agreed, but on the other hand, he hadn't been completely opposed. Wolff was confident he could win him over.

If Dulles was prepared to bring the proper Allied commanders to Switzerland, he would try to get Kesselring to meet with them within a week to sign the surrender.

Wolff also made it clear that he was operating on his own, without the knowledge of Hitler, Himmler, or anyone else in Berlin.

The meeting ended there. Nothing more could be done until Dulles contacted Washington, and until Wolff could win over Field Marshal Kesselring.

The day after the meeting, Dulles was informed by Allied Headquarters in Caserta, Italy, that Maj. Gen. Lyman L. Lemnitzer of the U.S. Army and the British Maj. Gen. Terence S. Airey were on their way to Bern—disguised as OSS sergeants. It was at this point that the entire operation was given the codename Operation Sunrise.

Then, however, Wolff ran into trouble back in Italy. Upon his return, he discovered that one of his aides, whom he trusted, had reported his trip to Switzerland to Ernst Kaltenbrunner, who was head of all of Germany's security forces, including the Gestapo. Kaltenbrunner ordered Wolff to stay out of Switzerland—or else. Kaltenbrunner had no illusions about Wolff's reasons for visiting Switzerland.

Why then did the Gestapo chief not arrest Wolff? One can only guess, based upon the evidence at hand. For one thing, the SS was a powerfully independent body. If Wolff chose to resist arrest, he might very well provoke open rebellion against Berlin with his own loyal troops. Furthermore, Wolff was a favorite of Hitler's. In the insane atmosphere of Berlin early in 1945, with Hitler unpredictable, a move against Wolff could have backfired right in Kaltenbrunner's face.

There remained one more possibility. Kaltenbrunner,

along with most high-ranking Nazis, knew the end was in sight. Along with these others, he might well have been hedging his bets. While protecting his rear by remaining loyal to Hitler, he quite probably thought it prudent to give Wolff a certain amount of leeway, to be seen by the Allies as a "cooperative" Nazi during the final hours of Hitler's Third Reich.

(It didn't help. Kaltenbrunner was hanged as a war criminal in October 1946, after the Nuremberg Trials.)

Meantime, while assuring Kaltenbrunner he would obey orders, Wolff told Dulles he was prepared to carry out his promises. But another hitch had developed. Field Marshal Kesselring had been transferred from Italy to the Western Front. His successor, Gen. Heinrich von Vietinghoff, was a soldier who lived "by the book," and would not easily be persuaded to make an independent decision.

On March 19, at Ancona, near the Italian-Swiss border, Dulles and his aides, along with Generals Lemnitzer and Airey, met with Wolff and his men to discuss the situation. After reviewing all the options, it was agreed to follow the suggestion put forward by Wolff: He would go to the Western Front and try to persuade Kesselring to surrender. If Kesselring agreed, Vietinghoff would fall into line, and perhaps other German generals would as well.

More than two weeks passed before Wolff was heard from again—two anxious weeks during which Dulles and the Allied generals feared the worst. Finally, through Parilli, Wolff got word to Dulles. He had seen Marshal Kesselring, and the Marshal appeared willing to let Wolff get on with the surrender, although he himself could not do so on the Western Front, where fighting was too bitter and Hitler too closely in command.

But there were new complications. Himmler had telephoned Wolff and told him bluntly that he knew of the contacts made with OSS. He was now giving Wolff a direct order not to leave Italy again. Furthermore, he implied a threat to Wolff's wife and children if the order was not obeyed. And daily reports from SS officers loyal to Himmler would be sent to Berlin, verifying Wolff's compliance.

To give Wolff due credit, he defied Himmler's orders, despite the threat to his family. To maintain contact with Dulles in Bern, he offered to hide an OSS radio operator within SS Headquarters in Milan. The bold plan appealed to Dulles. From the OSS base at Bari, in southern Italy, he recruited a brave young Czech named Vaclav Hradecky—codenamed Wally.

Quickly Wally was installed in a building on the Via Cimarosa in Milan, in an area restricted to SS units only. With marvelous irony, Wally was in a building devoted to SS counterespionage. There he was under the protection of Capt. Zimmer.

While in Milan as the contact man between Wolff and OSS Bern, Wally decided to make himself otherwise useful. One day he reported the location of Vietinghoff's headquarters, with an invitation to bomb it. This was promptly done, and Vietinghoff narrowly escaped death. Then Wally radioed that Mussolini was in Milan, staying at the Palazzo Governo. He suggested that the building be bombed, but asked that care be taken, since he himself was lodged just three hundred yards away.

OSS decided to decline the invitation. Killing Musso-

lini was not important enough to warrant the risk of killing Wally at the same time and otherwise endangering
the success of the secret surrender negotiations.

By mid-April, news from Wolff via Wally was more
encouraging. He was in telephone communication with
Marshal Kesselring, and a Luftwaffe general had joined
their group. At this point, two "agents provocateurs,"
quite probably sent by Berlin, appeared simultaneously
in Bern and in Italy, intent on sabotaging Operation
Sunrise. The first made an attempt to get through to
Dulles, claiming he represented Gestapo Chief Kaltenbrunner. Dulles stalled him by sending an aide to see
him in Zurich.

The other attempt was by an agent who appeared in
Genoa pretending to be an officer in British Intelligence.
He got word to Vietinghoff that future negotiations
should be conducted through the British only, and that
dealing with Dulles in Bern was useless. This frightened
Vietinghoff half to death, because whether or not the
man was truly a British agent, it meant that the "secret"
negotiations with OSS Bern were not so secret after all.
Vietinghoff, in a panic, wanted to expose the entire affair
to Berlin. Fortunately, Wolff managed to dissuade him.

Suddenly, after so much promise, Operation Sunrise seemed to fall apart. Wolff was ordered to Berlin—a
depressing blow. Then, a message to Dulles from Washington ordered him to break off all Operation Sunrise
contacts. The message hinted at complications with the
Russians who, for their own political reasons, preferred
that the Germans did not surrender to the British and
Americans in northern Italy. The Russians were hoping

that a fanatical last ditch stand by the SS in northern Italy would force the Anglo-Americans to call upon Red Army units for help, or for help from Marshal Tito, the Soviet-backed leader of guerrilla forces in Yugoslavia. This would give Russia a postwar sphere of influence stretching across the Adriatic Sea into the Mediterranean and up to the French border.

It certainly appeared that Operation Sunrise was dead.

And then, on Monday morning, the 23rd of April, came the astounding news from Swiss Intelligence that, Wolff, his adjutant, and Col. Viktor von Schweinitz, representing Vietinghoff, were on their way in to surrender all German armies in northern Italy, both SS and regular Wermacht.

Dulles was indeed in a pickle. Here ready to be wrapped up was everything Operation Sunrise wanted. But he was under strict orders from Washington prohibiting further contact with the Germans. Quickly Dulles radioed Allied Headquarters with the news of Wolff's arrival to surrender. At the same time he asked his Swiss colleagues to stall the Germans in Lucerne.

Wolff waited for two days, while cables flew back and forth across the Atlantic. Finally Wolff said he had to return to Italy, stating that he could not guarantee the actions of German or Fascist forces in his area if he were not there to keep them in line. But he delegated full authority to his adjutant to sign the surrender.

On his return trip to Switzerland, Wolff was caught in a villa near the Swiss border by Italian partisans and surrounded. Word of this got to Dulles. The OSS chief now found himself in the peculiar position of having to rescue an SS general from the hands of the partisans. If Wolff were taken and undoubtedly shot on the spot, the surrender of the German forces could not be implemented.

Accordingly, a rescue party was organized to free Wolff. The group, led by an American OSS agent known to the partisans, managed to get through to the villa. There they found Wolff, unharmed, but in full SS uniform. They advised him to change into civilian clothes if they were to get him safely through the partisan lines. Eventually Wolff was slipped through the partisans and over the border into Switzerland.

On the same day, Col. Schweinitz and Maj. Wenner, who was Wolff's adjutant, went to Caserta (Allied Headquarters) to sign the official surrender documents.

Now rapid communications were vital, but Wally, who had moved to the town of Bolzano with Wolff and Zimmer, was having trouble with his radio. When Headquarters at Caserta sent him, in code, the text of the surrender signed by the two Germans, he had trouble deciphering it. Wolff became suspicious, wondering if perhaps OSS Bern was going to renege on its deal.

That same night, the SS General's suspicions were further aroused when American bombers attacked Bolzano and narrowly missed his headquarters. Frantically, Wally radioed Bern to stop the bombings or the SS could not be held in check by Wolff; furthermore, the bombing endangered his own life. Nevertheless, Bolzano was bombed again. Fortunately for Wally and the entire Sunrise operation, the bombings stopped after that, and Wolff and his SS men were reassured.

It was now May 1. According to the surrender terms, Wolff had to accept them by 2 P.M. on May 2. No word came from Wolff on May 1. Then, on the morning of May 2, Wolff radioed that Marshal Kesselring had removed Vietinghoff from command because of his "betrayal." He had also ordered the arrest of other officers involved in the surrender. But, Wolff explained, he had himself talked on the telephone to Kesselring in the early hours of the morning. He had gotten Kesselring to rescind the arrest orders and agree to the surrender.

Hostilities in northern Italy would cease at 2 P.M.

At precisely 2 P.M., the Germans began to lay down their arms. The war in Italy was over.

Due to Operation Sunrise and the extraordinary efforts of OSS Bern, Station Chief Dulles, Gaevernitz, and all the rest involved in the operation, countless thousands of lives had been saved, thousands more saved from maiming and mutilation, and the industrial and art life of northern Italy saved from complete destruction.

Further, northern Italy had been spared the presence of Russian or Communist Yugoslavian troops, at a time when tension was already building up between East and West over postwar political alignments and the division of enemy territory. Had the battle there raged on and Russian troops advanced into Italy, there might well have been a partitioning there today, much as Germany was split after the war.

INFILTRATING GERMANY

Getting agents into Germany itself was a difficult business. The best intelligence that ever came out of there was obtained by high-level defectors, through Allen Dulles's Bern office, as described in the previous chapter. Useful information also came via diplomatic contacts maintained by OSS agents in such neutral posts as Stockholm, Istanbul, Madrid, and Lisbon.

There was no attempt to put an American agent into Germany until June 1944. Then one American officer and two Yugoslavs crossed the frontier on an intelligence and sabotage mission. They survived forty-four days until they were caught and killed.

There were a number of problems to be faced in sending agents into Germany. First was recruiting. Refugees from the occupied countries provided OSS London with willing recruits for France, or Norway, or Italy. But not very many refugees from Germany were physically or mentally suitable for field agents.

It was possible for OSS to send agents into France or into other occupied countries who were less than fluent in the native language, because they found a willing underground movement to help them, to give them cover and hiding. But there was no organized anti-Nazi movement within Germany. Indeed there were few enough Germans strongly enough anti-Nazi to help OSS in any way whatsoever. Those few who did exist and were not in concentration camps had no way to make contact with OSS in London. Rarely, in any case, were they in a position to cooperate.

The exceptions to this, of course, were those anti-Nazis in high places who worked through Allen Dulles in Switzerland. But these Germans worked on a lofty level, and their positions were so dangerous that no agent from outside Germany dared try to make contact.

So OSS London was finally forced to use German-speaking non-Germans to pose as foreign laborers for infiltration into Germany. Even these were scarce, and the result was the forced recruitment of lower-caliber agents, who turned in a lower-caliber performance.

Having found a few agents, OSS then faced the problem of dropping them "blind" into Germany; that is, without a reception committee of agents or underground fighters. Then, assuming that problem was overcome, the agents would find few, if any, "safe houses" to live in. Finally, assuming even all these problems were solved, the final one was how to provide communications.

The first problem was resolved by simply taking the risk and dropping agents "blind." In the last nine months of the war in Europe, thirty-eight two-man teams were dropped this way. Four teams were never heard from and presumed captured and killed. The false documentation carried by all the agents, their cover stories, and

their clothing proved good enough to let them survive—
with one exception.

The one problem that proved to be almost impossible
to overcome was communications. The situation in Germany made all previous communications systems useless.
In France and in other occupied countries, agents were
able to use wireless sets by operating from safe houses
and moving frequently to avoid the Gestapo's direction-
finding equipment.

In Germany a hostile native population and tighter
security made it difficult, if not impossible, for an agent
to carry around a wireless set, a power supply, aerials,
and a codebook. Three of the thirty-four teams sent during this period did carry wireless sets and used them successfully, only because they were dropped in the mountains of Austria, where there were known to be resistance
groups to protect them.

From Germany itself radio contact was made with
only four teams. This was accomplished by using a new
communications device known as the J-E system, nicknamed Joan-Eleanor.

The J-E system was a two-way device enabling the
agent on the ground to talk directly with another OSS
agent flying in a specially equipped plane above him.
The J-E equipment carried by the agent on the ground
was compact and light (four pounds), and so easily carried and concealed. Its use of long-life batteries eliminated the need for an outside power supply. The plane
flew at 30,000 feet, circling; at that height and with Allied mastery of the air over Germany, there was little
danger of Luftwaffe interference. There was also little
chance of enemy interception of the radio conversation,

and the high frequency and vertical cone-shaped directivity of the J-E device made it foolproof against direction-finders.

The J-E system was a tremendous development. Using it, an agent could transmit directly as much information in a twenty-minute conversation as would normally take two days to send via wireless. Furthermore, in a two-way conversation questions could be asked and vague information clarified. As a double-check all conversations were recorded on the aircraft.

To fly the Joan-Eleanor missions, OSS obtained three British "Mosquito" bombers. The tail sections were remodeled to take oxygen systems and the OSS operator with his equipment. The crews were given special training in the precision techniques necessary for the operations.

The system was a good one, but new, and it experienced teething problems. It also suffered from the inexperience of the ground agents. Communication required perfect timing. Both plane and ground agent had to be at a fixed rendezvous point at a certain time. But there were inevitably occasions when the plane met delay or when the agent found it dangerous to communicate. Later, it was learned that some of the agents mishandled the sets completely and made them useless.

For one reason or another, most of the Mosquito missions were in vain; no contact was made. Just four J-E teams in Germany operated successfully. These were team Hammer, in Berlin; team Pickaxe, in Landshut; team Chauffeur, in Regensburg; and team Luxe 1, in Weilheim.

The first J-E agent sent out in November 1944 was

actually sent to Ulrum, Holland. This was a lone agent, codenamed Bobby. His job was to lay the foundations for an underground railroad system which would infiltrate OSS agents from Holland into Germany. He was also told to gather whatever intelligence he could.

First contact with Bobby was made on November 21.

Two months later the Gestapo grabbed him and from the 10th of February until he went off the air he was under control of the Germans. By a strange quirk of fate, his capture was not due to German direction-finding equipment or his own failures, but to a case of mistaken identity.

Early in February the German security police arrested a group of Dutch resistance men. Under questioning the Dutch revealed that when picked up they were on their way to kill an Allied agent turned traitor—an agent codenamed Bobby. In fact, there was such an agent in the area, but it was not the J-E mission Bobby. The Dutch had made a mistake.

But the Gestapo arrested the J-E mission Bobby and told him they had just saved him from assassination by the Dutch underground; they believed him to be the other agent. Bobby caught on to the mistake in identity and played along. He acted fed up with the underground and with the Allies and agreed to help the Gestapo.

As soon as he got on the air again Bobby used his prearranged code signal—frequent use of profanity. OSS caught the signal and began their standard operation for keeping captured agents alive by sending him misleading or unimportant material to give the Germans.

In April the Germans sent Bobby through the lines with a message from the Gestapo to OSS, offering cooperation in a joint venture against Russia and Japan. So Bobby survived.

It was mentioned earlier that with one exception the documents and clothing of all the J-E ground agents proved to be perfect. This one exception was in the case of agent codenamed Adrian, on the Martini team. His harrowing story is worth repeating in detail, as a sample of what happened to an OSS agent caught by the Gestapo.

Shortly after landing and acquiring some good intelligence information, Adrian separated from his radio operator. He thought that for cover it would be a good idea to find work in his line. He spoke fluent German. He had—or so he thought—properly faked papers.

He went to the town of Augsburg and reported to the Eisenbahn Bureau (railroad). He asked for a job, saying he was from Poznan and had been sent to Augsburg to work on the railroad there. At the railroad office they checked his papers and sent him to another office. There Adrian realized he was in the office of the Kripo (Criminal Police).

They listened to his story and then demanded a *Marschbefehl* (travel order) from the authorities in Poznan. Adrian didn't have one. He told the Kripo that he had lost the paper. They seemed satisfied and gave him railroad tickets to proceed to the town of Halle, where he would find work. But they warned him to go to Halle immediately or he would be punished.

Instead of taking that train, he got on another train

which would take him to Ulm, where his radio operator
was waiting. But as he boarded the train two Kripo men
grabbed him, questioned him, and put him on the train
to Halle. He was guarded by two other Kripo men. At
Halle they escorted him to the railroad employment
office and waited outside.

Adrian told the railroad official his story about being
sent from Poznan. The official pulled out a list of all railroad workers registered in Poznan. His name was not
there. The official immediately threatened to call the police, but Adrian begged him not to and offered him a
bribe of 1,000 marks.

The official then gave him papers to work in Altenburg. Outside the office Adrian was again stopped by the
two Kripo men who demanded to know where he was
going. He showed them his work permit, and they then
put him on the train to Altenburg. There he reported to
the railroad office and was told to report to the local
police to register. (As the reader can see, security in Germany was so tight it was almost impossible for an ordinary citizen to go anywhere or do anything without
proper documents and official permission.)

Adrian's papers were checked and he was given food
ration cards and told to report to the *Wehrmeldeamt*
(draft board) because his soldier's book had expired.
Adrian went to the draft board where his papers were
checked once again, and it was noticed that on his draft
card the physical description had not been entered (a
lamentable lapse by London).

The draft board official examining his papers was a
sharp-eyed man. He then noticed that Adrian was forty-

one, single, and had never been in military service. Further, his citizenship was of a type that could be revoked (he was not given papers of a native-born German). The official knew that such a person could never have held an important railroad job, as Adrian claimed he had in Poznan.

The police were called quietly, while Adrian was kept waiting. When the police came, they immediately showed him a slip of paper with his name on it. They told him the Kripo had phoned to warn them to keep an eye on him because some of his papers were not in order. They took Adrian to the police station and held him in custody four days—until the Gestapo arrived.

During those four days Adrian managed to dispose of small bits of paper on which he had scribbled intelligence information. But he kept one large sketch of an airfield; he felt he might still bluff his way out of trouble, and the airfield sketch was important. But when he saw the Gestapo men he knew he was finished. They took him out of his cell and to the railroad station where they all boarded a train back to Halle. On the train, Adrian managed to chew the sketch bit by bit and swallow it.

At Gestapo headquarters in Halle they told him first to take off his shoes. They cut them up, layer by layer, looking for something incriminating. They then took off all his clothes and ripped them to pieces, but they could find nothing. After searching his body, they gave Adrian a hypodermic shot in the arm and in the hip and gave him a glass of some solution, which he refused to drink.

When he refused the drink, a Gestapo agent hit him in the face with the butt of a rifle, knocking out five teeth.

Then they forced the solution down his throat. It made him nauseous, and he vomited. But the Gestapo could see that he did not vomit everything, so they went to work on him again. He was stretched out face down on a table and two cylindrical rubber rollers were pressed against his body and rolled from his knees up to his ribs. During this process one man hit him repeatedly in the back with a rifle butt. Finally, the Gestapo men were convinced he had vomited the entire contents of his stomach.

The contents of Adrian's stomach were then examined with a large magnifying glass. Parts of the sketch were found. The Gestapo showed them to him and accused him of being a spy. Adrian denied it. He said the little bits of paper were from some candy he'd eaten, and from which he could not remove the paper. Of course, they didn't believe this.

For the next five days, for six to eight hours a day, the Gestapo beat Adrian with rubber clubs. He was given no food and only a little warm water with salt; if he drank it, he got sick again. The Gestapo insisted that he was a spy, or if not a spy, then a deserter from the army. Adrian would not say anything at all.

On the sixth day he was told he was either going to be shot or sent to Buchenwald concentration camp. A few hours later Halle was bombed by American B-17 Flying Fortresses. One bomb landed right next to the prison and blew out the doors of several of the cells. Since the Gestapo were all in underground shelters, Adrian and two other prisoners ran out and escaped.

He went off on his own, running as hard as he could. Despite his weakened condition he made it out of Halle to a small forest, where he finally collapsed. He slept in the forest until the next day. He then began walking through the forest and met a group of Russian and Polish slave laborers. They gave him some food and a place to sleep when he told them he was an army deserter and had been beaten up by the SS.

Adrian kept on walking aimlessly, until finally, on the 15th of April, he met an American Army patrol. He was taken to see a Maj. Clark, who believed his story. Adrian then remained with the Army, working with the Counter-Intelligence Corps, and had the satisfaction of helping them round up twenty Gestapo members in the area.

Looking over the prisoners, Adrian saw the two men who had tortured him. He snatched a pistol from an American officer's holster and shot both men dead.

A few days later he was sent on to an OSS unit at Weimar, and from there sent on to Luxembourg for a rest, until the OSS was eventually disbanded.

As the end of the war in Europe approached, OSS agents moved in behind the armies and established bases in some of the larger German cities, such as Bremen, Hamburg, Heidelberg, and Munich. These units served a number of functions. For example, X-2 agents worked to trace German funds and physical wealth to hideouts in neutral countries and on other continents, notably South America. Many high-ranking Germans had sent fortunes in cash and art objects out of the country when they knew the war was lost. Much, but not all of this, was recovered.

In March 1945, OSS agents parachuted near prisoner-of-war camps and persuaded a number of camp commanders to disobey orders that might have meant forced marches and massacres of Allied prisoners. These commanders agreed to surrender.

Other OSS agents, particularly from X-2, helped track down important Nazis gone underground. Often working with Army Counter-Intelligence, they unearthed SS officers and Gestapo agents and investigated reports of possible German resistance movements to the Allied occupation.

OSS contributed its extensive intelligence files to the American prosecutors at the war crimes trials, held in Nuremberg after the war. Gen. Donovan was appointed Associate Chief of Prosecution and other OSS agents served on the staff of Justice Jackson. They were able to contribute a substantial amount of written and photographic material on Nazi horrors, including captured German photos and films, that helped to prove the guilt of the high-ranking Nazis on trial.

Between the end of the war in Europe in May and the disbanding of OSS on October 1, 1945, agents gathered intelligence not only in the American-occupied zones, but in the zones occupied by the British, French, and Russians. A file was begun on Russian activities and policies. The Cold War was already sprouting.

Sprouting with it, despite its official termination at the end of September, was the seedling of a new, permanent U.S. intelligence organization, with new secret intelligence and new counterespionage objectives.

OPERATIONS IN THE FAR EAST: Burma

In the overall strategic planning during World War II, the defeat of Japan was given secondary importance by the Combined Chiefs of Staff. The main Allied effort was directed against Germany. Men and material for the war in Europe were given the higher priority. This of course affected the strength of U.S. military forces in the Far East. At the same time, it forced local military commanders to rely all the more on irregular methods of warfare and to make use of men and resources already available in those areas.

The techniques used successfully by the OSS in Europe could not be used in the Far East. The classic method of gathering intelligence in wartime, used in Europe, calls for the placing of agents first in neutral territory, then, where possible, into enemy territory. For example, OSS operated well in Switzerland, Sweden, Turkey, and Spain before penetrating occupied France and then Germany.

But there were no accessible neutral countries around

Japan. Further, OSS agents faced the tremendous handicap of racial differences. In Europe, an American could pass himself off as a Frenchman or an Italian or a German. Many OSS agents, either European-born or second-generation Americans, could speak a European language. Obviously, no American could exist and circulate among the Japanese or the Chinese or in the Japanese-occupied countries unless he was of Asian descent. For security reasons the use of Japanese-Americans was rejected; they just weren't trusted—an overreaction to Japanese treachery at Pearl Harbor. (But a Japanese-American regiment did serve brilliantly in Italy.)

Because of these conditions, because the theater of operations was sparsely populated and often a jungle, and because Japanese occupation forces were thinly spread, Special Operations tactics were called for. The Far East was ripe for guerrilla warfare.

Yet, although the Secret Intelligence functions of the OSS in this theater were limited, agents discovered political developments that in the long term were more significant than any of their Special Operations missions.

In Asia, as in Europe, there were two wars being waged at the same time: the one against the enemy by the Allies, and the one behind the scenes among the Allies themselves. Even as they fought the Japanese there was a cynical elbowing for postwar influence in Asia among the Allied nations. Perhaps this was true even more in the Far East than in Europe; here, in India, Indochina, and the island groups of the Pacific, there was a growing movement for independence from Britain and from France, the two principal colonial powers.

Thus France and Britain fought not only to drive the Japanese out, they fought to get themselves back in.

Meanwhile, in China, the Communists called a temporary truce in their battle against the regime of Chiang Kai-shek, in order to fight against Japanese occupation.

As the OSS became ever more deeply involved in its activities in the Far East, its officers saw beyond the purely military aspects of their missions. In carrying out assignments they found themselves enmeshed in inter-Allied politics time and time again. In China, though America supported Chiang in the common war against Japan, OSS officers assigned to the Dixie Mission made contact with Communist leaders Mao Tse-tung and Chou En-lai. They reported back to Gen. Donovan on developments within China.

The same story applied to Indochina. While the local populations cooperated in a guerrilla war against the Japanese, they continued to voice their long-held hopes for independence. OSS agents who penetrated the area and reported on political events spoke of meeting Ho Chi Minh and his warnings of a war of independence to come.

Postwar politics is beyond the scope of this book; nevertheless, the state of the world today can be better understood when the history of World War II is better understood. Thus a number of OSS reports from Vietnam and from the interior of China will be given later in this section. In the light of what happened in China and in Vietnam after the war, the wartime reports of the OSS from those areas come as a revelation.

From the outset the OSS was plagued by politics in

what was called, militarily, the China-Burma-India Theater. The Indian government was hostile to any OSS activities. The British government was equally hostile. The Chinese were happy to have OSS help, but only under their own command and only if the United States continued to supply them with money, arms, and supplies—which they used to fight the Communist forces under Mao Tse-tung.

As for the French, many of them who remained behind when the Japanese occupied the French areas of Indochina collaborated with the Japanese. In any event, the Free French under Charles de Gaulle made it clear that when the Japanese were driven out they intended to reclaim their colonies.

Such was the atmosphere in which the OSS was forced to operate.

The first unit to reach Asia arrived in India in the summer of 1942. It was to serve under the Commanding General of the CBI Theater, Gen. Joseph W. Stilwell, and was intended for use in China. But Stilwell changed its mission. A tough, crusty, independent commander, nicknamed by his men, "Vinegar Joe," Stilwell had two good reasons for changing the OSS unit's orders.

First, he felt that the kind of guerrilla warfare the unit was trained for could best be exploited not in China, but in Burma. Second, Stilwell felt that clandestine operations in China by the OSS would collide with operations there commanded by the U.S. Navy in cooperation with the Chinese Secret Police.

These naval activities were under the command of Capt. (later Rear Admiral) M. E. Miles, in close contact with Gen. Tai Li, director of China's internal security and counterintelligence service. Tai Li was actually the Director of the combined Sino-American service, with Capt. Miles his Deputy.

Stilwell did not like this arrangement. He believed in the complete independence of any OSS unit from foreign control, as did Donovan. Therefore, to avoid conflict with Capt. Miles and with Tai Li, he decided to keep this first OSS unit out of China. He called the unit Detachment 101.

The unit was established at a base camp near Nazira, in the province of Assam, not far from the Burma border. At the time, Stilwell's big job was the reopening of an overland supply route to China, from India. United States policy called for the support of Chiang's government and his armies in the field against the Japanese. Because of Japan's domination of the southwest Pacific, the only way to get substantial supplies through to China was via India, through Burma.

Early in the war, the Japanese advance into northern Burma cut the Burma Road approaches. They maintained four divisions in the country to keep China isolated.

To reopen a supply route was a monumental task. Burma, about the size of Texas, was covered with mountains and swamp and jungle. Roads were almost nonexistent. A major engineering feat would be needed to carry supplies over new roads. A further problem was that many of the 15 million Burmese were anti-British.

Stilwell's answer to the construction problem was the preparation of a new road which would eventually connect with the old Burma Road. This new road, first called the Ledo Road (later Stilwell Road), was to begin at Ledo on the Assam-Burma border, go through the Hukawng Valley south to Myitkyina in Burma, through the town of Bhamo in Burma, and eventually hook up with the Burma Road at the China-Burma border.

It was an ambitious plan (a film was eventually made about it). But before this road could get anywhere, the Japanese had to be cleared from Myitkyina and the whole northern Burma area.

Stilwell's first order to Detachment 101 was clear and concise: to deny to the Japanese the use of Myitkyina airfield, some 150 miles inside Burma, by means of sabotage and other means the Detachment might develop. It was absolutely vital that this airfield be neutralized to prevent Japanese fighter planes from attacking American supply aircraft flying into China and from attacking the men building the Ledo Road.

Late in December 1942, an advance party of fifteen OSS from Detachment 101 flew to northern Burma to establish a forward base at the town of Sumprabum. The men arrived first at Fort Hertz (the town of Putao) in two C-47 transport planes, with four fighter escorts. They were in British uniforms under cover of members of the Kachin Levies—a British Army unit. However, the British commander of the Levies had already informed Fort Hertz that Americans were coming.

That blew the OSS cover from the start. So the men said they were a Tenth Air Force radio unit. The attempt at a cover story was felt necessary since natives who worked as civilians for the British sometimes spied for the Japanese. In any case, the Japanese knew soon enough that something special was going on in northern Burma.

Shortly after their arrival at Fort Hertz the fifteen OSS men proceeded to Sumprabum, on a convoy of elephants. The fifty-mile trip took six days over the primitive jungle trails. It initiated the unit into the problems of Burmese field conditions, including the necessity to bribe the elephant handlers daily to keep them on the job.

At Sumprabum the unit ran into a command problem. The British commanding officer at Sumprabum demanded that the OSS operate under his direction. Unfortunately, this was not only against OSS policy, but self-destructive, since, according to the OSS reports, this commander seemed to change his mind every day, according to personal whim.

The OSS Detachment commander decided to get out of Sumprabum, leaving behind three men to run a radio station.

Eventually, when the Japanese began to push toward Sumprabum, the British abandoned the base and fell back behind the Indian border. But the OSS unit remained behind the lines, sending intelligence to the Tenth Air Force on bombing targets.

The Detachment made good use of the Kachins in northern Burma. These were small, wiry, dark-skinned tribesmen who lived in the area north of Myitkyina. They weren't particularly pro-British, but they remained loyal while most other Burmese tribes and groups went over to the Japanese.

The Kachins were by nature excellent soldiers. They understood guerrilla warfare; they were brave and strong and had tremendous stamina. The jungle and the difficult mountain terrain of northern Burma was their own backyard, and so they were perfect guides. Kachins and members of Detachment 101 were formed into "V-Forces," operating far ahead of regular Army units, raiding Japanese supply convoys, recovering downed American flyers, and performing reconnaissance for Army and Air Force units.

By November 1943 a substantial amount of progress had been made on the supply route to China, but the long rainy season in the area hindered operations. Dirt roads became impassable. Combat planes could not fly. Men became ill with dysentery and malaria. Myitkyina was still held by the Japanese.

With the dry season came a renewal of the Stilwell campaign in northern Burma. Ahead of the main forces there was to be a newly formed operational group, the 5307th Composite Unit, under Brig. Gen. Frank D. Merrill. This unit came to be known as Merrill's Marauders. (A film starring Jeff Chandler as Merrill was made about this unit's adventures in Burma.)

Detachment 101 was ordered to assist Merrill's men on the advance. The primary target was Myitkyina and its airfield.

[An interesting footnote to history: the formation of Merrill's Marauders was top secret. The unit was loaded onto a ship in San Francisco, and the ship "sealed." By chance an OSS agent, en route to the Theater, was also put on board this ship. For security reasons, no one was allowed to be detached from the Marauders. As a result the OSS agent, though completely untrained for combat, had to stay with the Marauders through several months of the extremely difficult campaign in Burma. He won a Bronze Star medal for his work with Merrill.]

On March 3, 1944, the Marauders hit the first Japanese defenses, and the long battle was on. This was no set-piece battle, as might take place in Europe. This was a battle of ambushes, of snipers hidden in trees, of stragglers being picked off by the knife, of booby-trapped jungle paths, of men dying silently at night in their foxholes, strangled with strands of wire.

Detachment 101 and its Kachins supported the Marauders all along the way, operating fifteen to twenty miles behind the Japanese lines. Kachin guides patrolled the flanks and kept Merrill informed of Japanese movements. Detachment radios called in air strikes and supplies. The Kachins cut trails through the jungle, built bamboo bridges, found water holes, and cleared fields large enough to take the L-5 planes used to evacuate the sick and wounded.

On March 15, 1st Battalion of the Marauders was hit by a large force of Japanese and almost surrounded. Unknown to the colonel in charge of 1st Battalion, he got help from a 101 unit called Lightning Force. This was a group of 200 Kachins led by an American lieutenant. They ambushed and harassed the Japanese battling the Marauders, and eventually established contact with the besieged battalion. Then, led by the Kachin guides, 1st Battalion escaped the Japanese net and continued on its march to Myitkyina.

Meanwhile, 2nd and 3rd Marauder Battalions were advancing through the Mogaung Valley. They were screened by a 101 unit called Knothead, consisting of eight Americans and 331 Kachins. The Knothead unit proved to be so aggressive and effective against the Japanese that the enemy was convinced a much larger force faced them. The Japanese backed off with caution, when a sustained attack with their greater numbers could have destroyed Merrill's force.

In April, still on the move, the Marauders were ordered to carry out a wide flanking movement. This was to be their most difficult maneuver, since they were to hit Myitkyina itself and take the airfield and the town. But by now the original Marauder force was seriously weakened. Battle casualties, illness, and exhaustion had taken their toll.

They had lost about 700 men of their 3,000. There were no American replacements for these casualties. Stilwell therefore decided to reinforce Merrill with men from Detachment 101, with Kachins and American-trained Chinese.

According to the plan of attack, Force Galahad, assisted by Force K, would make a surprise assault on Myitkyina airfield. This assault group was then led by group Pat, a 101 unit, on a devious course through rice paddies and thick jungle, to avoid detection by the Japanese or unfriendly natives. On May 15, just as the group neared its objective, the chief Kachin guide was bitten by a poisonous snake. Though racked with pain and fever, the guide insisted on leading the assault force the rest of the way.

Two days later Force Galahad struck at the airfield, catching the Japanese completely off guard. In a swift, fierce battle, the Japanese were overcome. The airfield was in American hands.

The commander of Galahad radioed to the Detachment 101 commander: "Thanks to your people for a swell job. Could not have succeeded without them."

But there remained the town of Myitkyina itself. Taking it required another ten weeks of tough fighting. While regular army units besieged the town, units of Detachment 101, codenamed Forward, prevented the Japanese from reinforcing the garrison. Along the whole of the left flank Forward elements harassed the Japanese. They took on an entire battalion and stopped them cold, keeping them out of the main battle. Finally, on August 3, Myitkyina fell.

South of this area, British Gen. Orde Wingate was leading a drive across central Burma. Detachment 101 furnished liaison and intelligence officers as well as guerrilla scouts for combat patrols on the flanks. By the end of the Burma campaign, Detachment 101 was given responsibility for all Allied clandestine activities in the area.

With Myitkyina in Allied hands, the first phase in the reopening of the Burma Road had been completed. But two other key points had yet to be cleared of Japanese— Bhamo and Lashio.

In October, the offensive was resumed. By now Detachment 101 had ten Kachin battalions under its wing, each composed of about 1,000 men. These battalions formed an arrowhead for the advancing British and

Chinese divisions, at the same time patrolling both flanks against enemy counterattack. At one point in the advance, agent codenamed Ski of the Detachment sent a warning to the commander of the British 36th Division that a battalion of Japanese was forming up for a surprise attack on the right flank.

The British were able to deploy for the attack and defeated it. Later, the British commander reported that agent Ski had "saved the Division."

For a period of six months in 1944, Detachment 101 forces were the only Allied troops between the Katha and the Chindwin Rivers. These rivers run north and south in the western part of Burma. The Allied high command was worried that the Japanese might be preparing an offensive in this area which would strike northward at the new Ledo Road.

Detachment 101 aggressively patrolled 100 miles of ground between the two rivers, keeping a Japanese division off balance and on the defensive, thinking in turn that an Allied offensive was coming. As a result, the Ledo Road was kept safe and the right flank of the British kept secure.

Bhamo was taken, and then Lashio, with Detachment 101 once again leading the way. So swift and mobile were they in their guerrilla attacks, that the enemy thought they were airborne troops. Obstacles were placed on every open field, and the Japanese commander warned his men to look out for American "airborne battalions."

Men from Detachment 101 were the first to hit the Japanese on the old Burma Road, attacking them between Wanting and Hsenwi. And 101 units were the first to enter Lashio itself, in February 1945. The Burma Road was open once again.

During these campaigns in Burma, it was estimated that Detachment 101 had inflicted 4,350 casualties on the enemy. Fifty-three Japanese were captured. OSS combat casualties consisted of just one American killed, 75 Kachins killed, and 125 Kachins wounded. Troops of 101 were also credited with guiding 228 Allied Air Corps personnel to safety after being shot down, and with evacuating 470 wounded American, British, and native troops by the 101 light plane squadron.

The official report on Detachment 101 in Burma concludes as follows:

"There is reason to believe that Detachment 101, the first United States unit to form an intelligence screen and to organize and employ a large guerrilla army deep in enemy territory, has made a significant contribution to the success of the military operation in Burma . . . The Detachment's efforts made it possible to fight the Japanese with more complete knowledge of enemy positions and movement than has been possible in most Theaters of this war.

"In the opinion of the Chief of Staff, the Detachment performed in an outstanding manner one of the most difficult and hazardous assignments that any military unit has ever been called upon to perform."

The members of Detachment 101 felt that the Kachin tribesmen deserved some official recognition for their loyal and courageous service. They requested that a special medal be approved for them. The Rear Echelon immediately prepared special medals for the Kachins, without getting authorization from Washington.

In their haste, the men in Rear Echelon misinterpreted the cable about the medal as asking for the CMA medal for the Kachins. But the CMA was actually the cable abbreviation for "comma"—cables being sent in all capital letters with no punctuation signs. (A period in a cable, for example, is the word, "stop.")

Hundreds of CMA medals were made and sent to forward 101 bases. The OSS men of the Detachment hastened to improvise. In dozens of Kachin villages they conducted impressive ceremonies, awarding to village headmen and faithful scouts the rare American decoration, the "Civilian Military Award."

When the news got back to Washington, officials at first ordered the medals returned. But it was soon realized that such action was impossible. As far as the Kachins were concerned, they were proud of their medals; there was no point in making them feel foolish by recalling them for being incorrect and unauthorized. This was certainly a case where it was the thought that counted, not the gift.

The Kachins kept their CMA medals.

Detachment 101 proved its ability to provide guerrilla support and intelligence in the North Burma campaign. It proved it so well, in fact, that when the campaign to reopen the Burma Road was concluded, the Detachment was given a combat mission to perform entirely on its own.

In April 1945, Lt. Gen. Sultan ordered Detachment

101 to clear the Japanese from the Shan States. This area was in eastern Burma, bordering Laos. The plan was to cut off all Japanese left in central Burma, eliminate all pockets of resistance, and prevent an enemy counterattack on the Burma Road.

Detachment 101 at this time numbered 3,200 men, most of them natives. Against them were 10,000 battle-hardened Japanese, equipped with artillery and tanks. Here, in the Shan States, the tactics used by the Detachment in northern Burma could not be used; there was no jungle, just barren hills of red dirt. Enemy artillery and armor could move swiftly. Detachment 101 had no artillery support or armor, but it did have the support of the 60th Fighter Squadron.

Splitting into four battalions, the Detachment assigned each battalion a specific combat zone, with orders to avoid a pitched battle. There was only one way to beat the enemy against the odds—hit-and-run, harass and confuse him, pin-prick him to death.

This is exactly what 101 did. One particular ambush by 1st Battalion typifies the action.

On May 17, a scout reported a party of 200 Japanese coming down the Lawksawk-Shwenyaung Road. Quickly the road was booby-trapped. Hand grenades connected by primer cord were hidden every three yards along a hundred-yard section of the road, while the ambush party took up positions at both ends.

The Japanese came marching down the road a few minutes later, with advance and rear guards of twenty-five men each. When the main body was inside the trap, the grenades were electronically detonated and the

guerrillas opened fire. For a full minute the firing continued into the mass of bewildered Japanese, then the
ambush party slipped off into the hills.

Not one man from the group was hurt. An estimated
one hundred Japanese were killed or wounded.

For weeks the men of the four battalions led the
enemy a merry chase. Time and time again they set up
small ambushes, shot up truck convoys, blew up bridges,
cut communications lines, and generally made life miserable for the Japanese. Bit by bit, the Detachment was
cutting them to pieces.

One battalion (the 10th) so harassed the enemy that
it invited a major counterattack. Five hundred Japanese
supported by artillery mounted an assault against the
battalion headquarters area. The guerrillas retreated
slowly, drawing the enemy on, mauling him with lightning raids. They kept this up for three days, remaining
just out of reach, until the Japanese, suffering heavy
casualties, gave up the chase.

Meantime, 2nd and 3rd Battalions were doing their
share of fighting, forcing the Japanese out of their defensive positions, then punishing them as they retreated.
The 60th Fighter Squadron did an extraordinary job of
coordination during this campaign. Detachment agents
operating behind enemy lines called down strafing and
bombing strikes on enemy convoys and fixed positions,
destroying pillboxes and concrete bunkers.

By June 15 the mission of Detachment 101 was completed. All Japanese pockets of resistance had been
wiped out. The last few remaining enemy troops had
withdrawn across the Burma-Laos border. There was no

longer a threat to the Burma Road. By this date in fact, the war in Europe had ended, and most senior Japanese commanders knew that the defeat of Japan was inevitable.

On July 12 Detachment 101 was officially deactivated. Some of the men were transferred to China, the rest were reassigned to other units or returned to the United States. Responsibility for Burma was turned over to the British Civil Affairs Service.

THE FAR EAST:
Vietnam

It is possible to write an entire book on the history of Vietnam since the end of World War II. Indeed, volumes have been written on the subject. America's long and sad involvement in the violence is a painful chapter in that history. In the light of America's part in what was called, at various times, by various people, a "civil war" or a "war for independence," it is important to know some of the background of the struggle.

Only recently has some of this background, some of this early history, been revealed. It turns out that the OSS was there, in what was then French Indochina, during the final weeks of World War II. Furthermore, OSS agents stayed on for months after the war was over, with the specific purpose of reporting back to Washington what was happening.

The reports by OSS officers make fascinating reading. It is not the purpose of this OSS history or the purpose of the author to make moral or political judgments on the actions of the United States in Vietnam. But considering the contents of these reports, parts of which appear below, one cannot help but wonder how and why the American disaster in Vietnam ever happened.

As World War II drew to an end in the summer of 1945, OSS agents in the Far East leapfrogged into the forward areas ahead of everybody else. The idea was to hasten the surrender of isolated Japanese garrisons and free American prisoners of war as soon as possible. OSS teams were also ordered to look after American property, evacuate American civilians freed from internment camps, and provide general intelligence.

Relations with the British began to deteriorate, at least at the higher levels. The British (and the French) did not welcome OSS teams into what they considered to be imperial zones of interest. The British, in fact, insisted that the final, formal surrender by the Japanese in that area should be to their Commander, Lord Louis Mountbatten. They got their way.

But attempts to get the OSS out of the way failed. The State Department and the Chiefs of Staff insisted that the United States had the right to firsthand knowledge of what was going on in the area. The OSS remained. One team, which had been on a Special Operations mission codenamed Operation Deer, was already in North Vietnam. This group, led by Maj. Allison K. Thomas, was working with a guerrilla force led by a man they knew as C. M. Hoo. This turned out to be Ho Chi Minh.

A brief background note on Ho Chi Minh is required here.

Ho was born in northern Vietnam in 1892. He had long been a "revolutionary" in a country that had been

battling for its independence from the French since
1885. There had been periodic wars between times of
peace. When World War II broke out and the Japanese
occupied all of Indochina, Ho was Chairman of the
Viet Minh League, which opposed the French. Under
Japanese rule, Ho remained underground, resisting the
occupation. In 1942, he went to China. As soon as he
crossed the frontier the Chinese arrested him and put
him in prison. This presumably was because he was
against the regime of Chiang Kai-shek, and in sympathy
with Mao Tse-tung.

After thirteen months in a Chinese prison, Ho was re-
leased so that he could organize the guerrillas around
Hanoi, in the northern half of Vietnam, and assist the
OSS. The OSS team, on Operation Deer, was to cross the
China-Vietnam border near Tsingsi, on the Chinese side,
and meet with a party of Viet Minh guerrillas near the
village of Kimlung, in Vietnam. With the OSS team were
French officers.

On June 19, 1945, Maj. Thomas received an OSS message warning him that if he crossed the border into Vietnam with any Frenchmen, he would not be made welcome. He would find the entire population against them
and would get no food. "Natives hate French" said the
message.

Maj. Thomas was disturbed by this message, but not
overly surprised. It was the second message to that effect
he had received from OSS Headquarters. Accordingly,
when preparations had been made for a parachute jump
into Vietnam, Maj. Thomas decided to take just one
French officer along on the small advance party, a Lt.

Montfort. This officer would see for himself the reception given and would report back to the French waiting in China.

Maj. Thomas led a six-man jump party into Vietnam on July 16. They landed in rice fields and were welcomed by a reception committee of Viet Minh guerrillas. The men were escorted to a small village, through a bamboo archway reading, "Welcome to our American friends." Then Maj. Thomas was introduced to "Mr. Hoo," whose true identity he did not then know.

While in the Viet Minh camp preparing for sabotage and guerrilla activities against the Japanese, Maj. Thomas and Ho Chi Minh (still as Mr. Hoo) discussed the problem of the French. The author here quotes from the original report made by Maj. Thomas to the Chief of OSS, Special Operations, on September 17, 1945. The report is on the Deer mission. Maj. Thomas describes in detail the organization of the mission and its adventures until his six-man party dropped near Kimlung and was escorted to the Viet Minh camp. Then he goes on:

> Held long conference with Mr. Hoo (Ho Chi Minh), on the subject of the French. He stated that the Vietminh Party, or League, was an amalgamation of all the political parties organized for the sole purpose of ousting all foreign powers and was working for the liberty and complete independence of Indochina. It had no political ideas beyond that as its members come from all political groups. After liberty had been achieved, then they would worry about politics. He definitely tabooed the idea that the party was communistic. He stated that at least 85% of the people of Tonkin (Ed. note: North

Vietnam) were members or sympathetic with its aims. It would be obvious to the most ordinary observer that the peasants didn't know what the word communism or socialism meant—but they did understand liberty and independence.

Consequently, Mr. Hoo made it very clear to me that it would be impossible for Lt. Montfort, the French officer, to stay, nor would any more French be welcome. He pointed out many grievances his people had against the French and many of his people hated them worse than the Japs. In fact, everyone talked against the Jap Fascists and French Fascists with equal fervor. He said he would welcome a million American soldiers to come in but not any French even though they were soldiers and insisted that they were here to fight Japs only, because as Mr. Hoo maintained it would only be an opening wedge for them.

He indicated he would gladly escort Lt. Montfort safely back to the frontier as he had done many other Frenchmen. . . .

Maj. Thomas and his men began to train the Viet Minh for further guerrilla action against the Japanese. The principal target was to be the town of Thai Nguyen, the provincial capital. But by the time the guerrillas were ready for a major action, the Japanese had surrendered (August 15, 1945) and the war was over.

When he got this news, Maj. Thomas wired back to his headquarters in Poseh, China, that he and his men could easily obtain the surrender of all the Japanese in the area. To his disappointment, he was told that under no circumstances was he to accept any Japanese surrenders. Maj. Thomas decided that since in any case there was no point remaining in the jungle, he would march his men to Thai Nguyen to await further developments.

Ho Chi Minh then said to him that he would like to remain in Indochina as long as possible—he had only been released from the Chinese prison to fight the Japanese. This was a request Maj. Thomas had no authority to grant. He told Ho he would have to check with his superiors. He was not optimistic. He told Ho he doubted that this was possible, since his party was not recognized, and his country not yet independent.

Maj. Thomas then set out for Thai Nguyen with a force of Viet Minh led by a "Mr. Van." This was the name used then by Vo Nguyen Giap, the number one Viet Minh general.

It is worthwhile here to note that the Japanese at Thai Nguyen had been in touch with Ho Chi Minh by letter, hoping to convert him to the Japanese cause. The following is an exact recreation of the letter sent by the Japanese. The author has made only a few corrections in spelling for clarity, since the original letter was obviously typed on a foreign typewriter with the letter "K" missing. The Japanese letter:

Jap Army at THAINGUYEN to the VML

These last 5 weeks, you often destroyed our trucks going between Tuyenquang and Thainguyen, and you hold the villages. Thus, the communication between these two provinces become disturbed and the population getting restless.

The Japanese army believes that you know such act is harmful to the population and to you. The population is frightened, the bandits—under the name of VML —are robbing everywhere, dishonoring the VML which is a real patriotic party.

We never consider you as our enemy, but always respect you as true patriotics who work sincerely to free their fatherland, Vietnam.

Now we drived out the French, and sincerely help the Vietnam people to realize their independence and to build up their country deserving her position as a nation in the Greater Asia.

From the beginning, you did not understand our sincerity, and you always organize anti-Jap movement. You must consider carefully. Only Japanese can help you realizing your hope. Hoping England or AMERICA to save Vietnam from the French hands, has the same sense as saving the Vietnam people from sunburn by throwing them into the fire.

In order to keep peace and order in Tuyenquang and Thainguyen, we are force to use armed troops against your senseless activities. But before sending out our troops, we sent you this letter, asking you to stop immediately the destruction of roads between these two provinces. If you stop destruction, we will stop sending troops against you. If you don't listen to our advice, it will then happen heartbreaking things: the Yellow men killing the Yellow men, and you will find yourselves in miserable situation. That is what both we and you don't want.

> Signed: Jap Headquarters at Thainguyen
> April 11, 1945

At the same time, two other factions in Vietnam were agitating against Ho Chi Minh and the Viet Minh guerrillas. According to detailed OSS reports, these were a political group called the Dai Viet, and a number of mandarins (provincial governors) who obviously stood to lose their jobs if the Viet Minh took over the country. The appeal to the people by both groups was similar to that sent out by the Japanese. From documents obtained by the OSS in the spring of 1945, here are excerpts from propaganda material of these two groups:

> "Appeal of Society of the People of Indo-China"
> (Second self of Dai Viet) against VML
> Patriot Countrymen!
> Who are the traitors who sell out our country to the White skin people? They are the VM who accept large sums of money from America, England and France . . .
> Thanks to the help from the Japanese Army, our country becomes independent. But to keep that independence we must help the Japanese army to win this war . . . Don't listen to the VML, who push you to fight against the Japanese . . . To listen to the VML is to suicide ourselves . . .

> A proclamation from "The Mandarins of Thainguyen to the VML"
> 80 years of oppression.
> All our countrymen suffered.
> By patriotism you sacrificed your lives to the independence of our country. Now, the Japanese arms has driven out the French and won back that independence for us. They sincerely help us in everything . . . Why do you keep on dividing so that the work of building the country becomes more difficult? . . .

Declaration of Nguyenbinh district official

1. The villagers cooperate with the communist bandits, destroying roads, cutting telegraph wire, fighting the Japanese army. All those who participate in that work will be sentenced to death, and their house burned.

2. Those who see the communist bandits must immediately inform the Japanese army.

3. The population must obey the order of the Japan army, go home, and work their rice field peacefully.

4. All villages of this district must obey this order. The villagers must come back to their ordinary life. The aim of the Japanese army is to give you peaceful life.

Within 5 days limit all must come home.

April 1945

The summary of OSS reports from Vietnam in the months preceding the Japanese surrender points to the fact that Ho Chi Minh's guerrillas were the only ones aiding the Allies and fighting the Japanese. Furthermore, the hatred of the large masses of Vietnamese for their French masters was such that it was possible to get them to accept Japanese occupation peacefully.

OSS field reports did indicate that by and large the Japanese occupation forces treated the Vietnamese people better than they were treated as French colonials. (When Maj. Thomas's group and the Viet Minh reached Thai Nguyen, the Japanese refused to surrender. This was an experience met by other Allied troops shortly after the end of the war. The Japanese soldier had for years been taught that to surrender was a terrible shame, that it was better to die in battle.

For this reason, all through the war, few Japanese

prisoners were ever taken. Most fought to the death. Some even committed suicide rather than be taken alive as a prisoner. For months after the war Japanese troops isolated on islands throughout the Pacific had to be hunted down and persuaded to surrender by fellow Japanese. In several cases Japanese soldiers hid out for years in the jungle.)

At Thai Nguyen, Maj. Thomas did not want to get his men involved in a shoot-out with the Japanese. He was also under orders to avoid a fight. But the Viet Minh had no such reservations. When the Japanese refused to surrender, they attacked the village. The battle lasted for four days—fortunately for both sides, there was more noise than casualties. No one was killed, a few slightly wounded. Finally the Japanese captain in command of the garrison surrendered.

After resting at Thai Nguyen, the entire group went on to Hanoi, where an OSS mission under a Capt. Patti was already installed.

This is how Maj. Thomas described the scene he found at Hanoi:

> Viet Minh flags were flying from almost every house. Banners were stretched across the streets with various slogans in Annamese (Vietnamese), English, Chinese, Russian, Indian, etc. French was noticeably absent.
>
> Some of the slogans seen everywhere were as follows: "Welcome Allies," "Welcome Peace Commission," "Down With French Imperialism," "Let's Kick Out French Imperialism," "Independence or Death," "2,000,000 people died under French domination," "VIETMINH FOR THE VIETNAMESE."

The Viet Minh Party at Hanoi had set up a Provisional Government and issued a "Declaration of Independence."

Our friend of the forest, Mr. C. M. Hoo, now Mr. Ho Chi Minh, was President of the Provisional Government and Minister of Foreign Affairs. Another friend of the forest, Mr. Van, now Vo Nguyen Giap, became Minister of Interior. Party members were appointed cabinet members. The new government appears to be enthusiastically supported by the majority of the population in every province of Indo-China. The new government was given strength by the resignation and abdication of Bao Dai, former puppet Emperor, who offered his services as friend and advisor.

The people know the French intend to come back but they keep saying if they come back with arms they will fight to the death . . .

From Hanoi, Ho Chi Minh issued the following proclamation:

5 Sept. 1945

Fellow Countrymen!

The Vietnamese people heartily welcome the Allied forces which are entering our territory in order to disarm the Japanese.

However, we are determined to oppose the moving in of the French elements, because their dark aim is to reestablish the French rule over our Fatherland.

Fellow countrymen!

At the present moment a few Frenchmen have managed to filter into our territory. The Government expects every man to fight for our liberty and independence.

President Ho Chi Minh

According to agreements made by the Allied powers, French Indochina, or Vietnam, was to be divided in two at the war's end, with the 16th Parallel the dividing line. Below the line, the British would take over; above the line the Nationalist Chinese. This was to be an interim arrangement until the status of the country could be worked out.

The above agreement was made on behalf of the United States by President Franklin D. Roosevelt, in concert with the other Allied leaders. It was President Roosevelt's stated intention that Vietnam not be returned to France after the war. It was the President's plan that an international trusteeship be set up for Vietnam, at least temporarily, pending complete independence.

But there were strong elements in the U.S. State Department which did want the French back in Vietnam. When these people tried to get the President to change his mind, he was adamant. He sent the State Department a cryptic note, saying, "No French help in Indochina."

However, President Roosevelt died before the war ended. When Harry Truman, then Vice-President, took over as President, this policy changed. Why and how the policy changed is a complex matter of government and politics outside the scope of this OSS history. But that is what happened.

The OSS file on events in Vietnam at the close of World War II, and in the months that followed, is a voluminous file indeed. OSS officers remained in Hanoi and in Saigon for a long time after the war, long after the OSS had been officially disbanded. Their reports appear to be unanimous in their appraisal of Ho Chi Minh and the Viet Minh as pro-American and nationalist.

These same reports, commenting on their communist affiliations, indicate no connections with either the Soviet Union or with the Chinese Communists. These reports are much too lengthy to quote here. The author recommends that any reader interested in probing deeper read *Causes, Origins, and Lessons of the Vietnam War,* mentioned in the bibliography.

THE FAR EAST:
China

The Chiefs of Staff of the United States armed forces considered China to be a secondary theater of war. They felt the best thing to do there in the short term was use the Chinese to keep the Japanese busy; tie down as many Japanese troops as possible with the minimum cost in American men and supplies. In the long term they wanted to see China replace Japan as the big postwar power in the Far East.

When the United States entered the war, Japan and China had already been battling for several years. The Japanese occupied and controlled the coastal areas of China, including the industrial centers, the major roads and railroads, and the major cities.

The Chinese National Government was run by Generalissimo Chiang Kai-shek, from the city of Chungking. But the northern area of China was under the control of the Chinese Communists, led by Mao Tse-tung and Chou En-lai. The Communists had declared a truce in their war against Chiang, to turn their attentions to the

Japanese. However, Chiang considered the Communists more of a threat than the Japanese. Particularly when the United States entered the picture, he put more men in the field against the Communists than he did against the Japanese.

Accordingly, when the OSS was first sent into China, its agents found it difficult to mount operations against the Japanese. Chiang and his generals were using most of their American arms and equipment to fight Mao and were little interested in what was supposed to be the common enemy. Chiang was confident that America would beat the Japanese without his help, so he felt free to pursue his own private war, within his own country.

In China, too, OSS agents found obstacles similar to those found elsewhere during the war. The Chinese, no different from America's other Allies, wanted OSS help, but they wanted it under their control. They objected strongly to an independent OSS operation in China, and in the beginning, they got their way.

The OSS found the Nationalist Chinese Army to be badly trained, inefficient, corrupt, and without motivation. It was incapable of taking the offensive against the enemy. Therefore, the only form of aggressive action possible was guerrilla activity and clandestine operations. This, then, became the primary task of OSS agents in Nationalist China. It was also important, however, to collect as much intelligence as possible on the Japanese. To get this, agents needed access to the Communist Chinese areas. Chiang did not want this to happen, and for a time blocked all contact. When contact was eventually made, OSS agents found themselves in a most delicate position: any deal with one side was met with hostility and suspicion by the other, and, further, any help given the Communists had to be considered as aiding a revolutionary party against a world-recognized government. One can be sure that Chiang made this point most strongly to the powers that were in Washington.

As explained in the previous chapter on the China-Burma-India Theater, the Chinese had an intelligence operation of its own, under Gen. Tai Li. But this had little to do with operations against the Japanese. It was used primarily to spy on dissident Chinese and anybody else who might give aid to the Communists. This was why, again, as mentioned earlier, Gen. Stilwell diverted the first group of OSS agents destined for China to Burma, as Detachment 101. He knew they would be useless in China.

But Gen. Donovan needed a foothold for the OSS in China. To get it, he compromised. In April 1943 he agreed to let the OSS in China operate within the framework of a new organization called SACO—the Sino-American Cooperative Organization. Tai Li was its director and U.S. Navy Capt. Miles its deputy director.

According to OSS reports, the Chinese contribution to SACO was thoroughly inefficient and corrupt; the defeat of the Japanese was only a minor concern to Tai Li. The only way OSS could get him to operate against the Japanese was by a mixture of bribes and threats. If he did as OSS asked, he was rewarded with valuable U.S. military supplies, to dispose of as he saw fit. If he refused to cooperate, OSS threatened to withdraw from SACO and set up in business on its own. To Tai Li, this would mean losing "face"—not to mention military aid.

The obstructionist attitude of Tai Li to the OSS knew

no bounds. He did everything he could to resist the growth and efficiency of the agency. He claimed that he had 400 intelligence stations throughout China, and his reports, which went straight to Capt. Miles, were good enough. Miles, on his part, did not give OSS any information until what he got from Tai Li had already reached Washington via his office.

To beat this delay, OSS asked Tai Li for copies of the reports he sent Miles. Tai Li said he couldn't do this, because the Chinese did not use carbon paper, and he had no way to make copies of the reports.

On another occasion, OSS offered to finance combined operations in Japanese-held territory. But the first time they made a concrete offer to Tai Li, he said he needed one million dollars to do the job, and it had to be an exclusive Chinese operation. No OSS could go along, he said, because if any agents were killed, he would be held responsible. That was the end of that idea.

For its own reasons, the Navy sided with Tai Li against the OSS. In effect this meant that SACO was run by the Chinese. It also meant that OSS agents operated under the control of Chiang Kai-shek, rather than its own Chief of Staff in Washington or under Gen. Donovan. As a result, the first eight months of SACO were useless. No worthwhile intelligence was gained, no guerrilla activities launched.

Gen. Donovan kept applying the pressure for an independent OSS in China. He realized that if he was forced to operate with his hands tied under the SACO agreement, he would just have to find a way around the agreement. So Gen. Donovan himself went to China, to test, as it were, the prevailing winds. What he found was a willing ally in Gen. Claire L. Chennault, Commander of the 14th United States Army Air Force (at that time there was no separate U.S. Air Force; it was part of the Army).

Chennault was badly in need of tactical ground-air intelligence; this meant he needed information on targets worth hitting, such as convoys, supply dumps, troop formations, and headquarters areas. Such information could only be obtained by intelligence agents working on the ground. He was getting absolute zero from SACO, because Tai Li's men were too busy spying out Communists, and because OSS agents were not allowed to roam around on their own.

In December 1943, therefore, Chennault and Donovan got together in Chungking and hatched out a plan. OSS agents would be assigned to Chennault's Air Force command and work under him, instead of SACO. As an experiment, two agents went to work for Chennault, gathering intelligence on targets, weather, and anything else they could find.

It worked beautifully. The information provided by these two agents alone was so useful to Chennault that he was able to persuade the Theater Commander, Gen. Stilwell, to set up an expanded, permanent, OSS-14th Air Force unit. This was called the 5329th Air and Ground Forces Resources and Technical Staff—AGFRTS, popularly known as Agfighters. The original unit was expanded to include twenty-four officers and thirteen enlisted men.

As a snub to Tai Li, he was never formally notified of the formation of this new unit, although of course he found out about it. But there was nothing he could do. The prestige of Chennault and the 14th Air Force was too great. Chennault himself was a folk hero in China. Long before the United States entered the war he had helped the Chinese with his air force organization called the Flying Tigers—unofficially, of course, not as a United States officer.

AGFRTS succeeded where SACO failed. Operating under its cover as an Army Air Force unit, it was actually an OSS organization. The results were felt immediately. All branches of the OSS swung into action—Secret Intelligence, Special Operations, and Counter-Espionage, foremost among them.

Agents slipped through the lines and set up clandestine radio stations in enemy territory. Soon they began reporting back to headquarters in the town of Kweilin. Daily "hot" flashes on spot targets were sent to fighter-bomber bases. Reports were sent on weather conditions, bombing results, enemy morale, troop movements, and river traffic.

In addition, agents rescued downed airmen and sabotaged supply depots, railroads, and communications; they deceived the enemy by allowing "secret reports" to become "lost" or "stolen" by Chinese known to be Japanese agents.

Perhaps one of the most important accomplishments, in the long view, was the penetration of Communist-held northern China. This came about with the Dixie Mission, still under AGFRTS cover, since Tai Li would not allow OSS agents into Communist areas. The Dixie Mission will be discussed in detail later in this chapter.

At the end of October 1944, Lt. Gen. A. C. Wedemeyer

assumed command of the China Theater. By now the situation of Chiang's government was critical. The Chinese military campaigns the previous summer had ended in disaster; 700,000 Chinese troops in Hunan Province had been defeated by just 100,000 Japanese. At the same time, the strength and popularity of the Mao-led Communists was growing steadily.

Gen. Wedemeyer was given a two-fold task: to support the Chinese Nationalist Government and armies with supplies and training and to maintain intelligence and guerrilla activities against the Japanese.

In Washington, meanwhile, Gen. Donovan was fighting for OSS independence in China. He met with President Roosevelt and told him bluntly that Chiang and the Chinese government had blocked all efforts by the OSS to establish itself. He pointed out that SACO gave him and his men no cooperation. He said to the President:

"I discussed this situation with you before my last trip to China. You agreed with me that we could not do our job unless we operated as an independent organization. You authorized me to tell the Generalissimo [Chiang Kai-shek] we must be permitted independence of operation . . ."

Gen. Donovan went on to explain how, under cover of the 14th Air Force, OSS agents had been able to provide excellent intelligence and sabotage operations. But it was not enough, Gen. Donovan said. He needed a completely free hand.

President Roosevelt gave it to him. The OSS was made completely independent, under the command of Gen. Wedemeyer.

With reorganization, OSS sent more men into China to

beef up its staff, and its activities moved into high gear. Special Operations took over training of guerrilla forces, with marked success. At times they operated as deep as 500 miles behind enemy lines. The basic field unit consisted of four OSS agents and 150 OSS-trained guerrillas.

Considering the terrible state of the Chinese armies, there was little the OSS could do by way of offensive action on a grand scale. But their guerrilla units, once they got them trained, did a fair job of harassment. When the Japanese drove on Liuchow, for example, two OSS teams led the Chinese in a spirited defense, destroying bridges and river ferries, setting up road blocks, and accounting for some 3,000 Japanese casualties.

One OSS team and its guerrillas accounted for the cutting of the railroads in 1,124 places, cutting telephone and telegraph lines in 156 places, the destruction of seven bridges, and the derailment of two troop trains. This same team repeatedly ambushed convoys and eventually was credited with inflicting more than 1,000 casualties.

Special Operations agents worked closely with the 14th Air Force. During the Japanese advance on Changsha, two OSS agents took a heavy toll of the enemy via its contact with a fighter-bomber base. Sighting an armored cavalry unit crossing a river near the village of Yi-Yang, the agents called in a strike. The fighter-bombers caught the Japanese in mid-river and wiped out almost the entire column.

Two days later these same agents repeated their success. They sighted Japanese troops crossing the Siang River in sampans for an attack on the village of Yolo Shan. The agents radioed this information to the 14th

Air Force. Within minutes fighter-bombers were attacking the sampans, which turned out to be double-decker troop barges. Some 23 barges were sunk, more than 1,000 Japanese troops killed and wounded.

Until OSS became independent at the beginning of 1945, the Secret Intelligence unit in China was almost useless, tied in knots by Tai Li and the SACO operation. True, when agents began to operate under cover of the 14th Air Force, it broke out a bit from its bonds and gained some useful intelligence (as in the Dixie Mission). But in the few months between the beginning of 1945 and the end of the war in August, Secret Intelligence showed what it could really do, given its head and given enough agents.

New teams penetrated Japanese lines throughout southern China, in the Shantung Peninsula, the Yellow River Bend area, the Canton-Hong Kong area, Shanghai and vicinity, Peiping (now Peking), and Tientsin, the area extending from Canton to the Indochinese border. In coastal regions OSS spies reported on ship movements, enemy air traffic, and troop dispositions. One major coup was the stealing of a list of Japanese Army Postal Code designations.

This list contained the designations of new military units, as well as those already in China. More than 400 Japanese postcards and letters identifying enemy units were taken. With this information, the Theater Commander could identify and locate the Japanese forces, such as the 133rd Division, the 129th, the 131st, and the shift of the 27th and 40th Divisions from central China to the Canton area.

Another major Secret Intelligence coup was the steal-

BEHINDENEMYLINES

ing of the code used by the Japanese Navy around the Shanghai area. This proved to be extremely valuable to the U.S. Pacific Fleet and its carrier-based planes, as well as to the 14th Air Force. At the special request of Gen. Wedemeyer, an OSS team spent two months surveying the Chinese coast from Hong Kong to Hainan, in preparation of a planned invasion. The dropping of the atomic bombs on Hiroshima and Nagasaki, of course, made this invasion unnecessary.

In the area of counterintelligence, the story was similar. As long as X-2 agents had to work under Tai Li and SACO, they accomplished nothing. A report by counterintelligence to Gen. Donovan on this problem said that Chinese efforts were "expended much less in preventing Japanese espionage penetration than in their own jurisdictional disputes and in spying on the Communists, Americans and British."

The problem was made more complex by the fact that even if an OSS agent did uncover an enemy agent, he could not make an arrest; he could do nothing but report his discovery to the Chinese, who might—or might not—decide to do something about it.

As soon as OSS went independent, the picture changed. X-2 organized a system of native agents at several field stations, since it was practically impossible for an American to carry on counterespionage because of racial and language barriers. The arrangement worked well. The agents infiltrated occupied China and in some cases worked their way into employment by the Japanese, thus becoming double agents.

The work of X-2, once established on its own, exposed

a Japanese network of agents in Asia assigned to espionage and assassination of important figures. In the spring of 1945, X-2 broke up three large enemy spy rings and caught 175 agents. In breaking up this ring, X-2 discovered that the agents were dealing in the drug traffic as well as espionage; further, plans were discovered for an assassination attempt against Gen. Wedemeyer and Chiang Kai-shek.

As the war wound to an end, X-2 unearthed espionage training schools, the leaders of the Japanese secret service in China, and even a German transmitting station in Canton which had agents spying for the Japanese and for Germany. X-2 captured the key German agent in China, Fritz Wiedemann, who before the war was German consul-general in San Francisco.

By war's end, X-2 had compiled a 15,000-card master file of agents, suspects, collaborators, secret societies, codes, and plans. Among these plans was one for a continued Japanese presence in China after the war (most high-level Japanese knew well in advance that they could not win the war).

According to OSS reports, the Japanese had made a deal with Chiang Kai-shek to help him fight the Communists. The plan went along these lines:

At a certain stage in the war, the Japanese would move their armies and entire industrial plants into certain selected cities. Chiang would then declare these cities "open cities," not to be attacked. The Japanese Army would oppose the entry of any Communist forces into these cities and put down any uprisings. They would then surrender to Chiang's troops.

At the same time, Japanese forces would hold onto all

lines of communication until Chiang's men could take over. In this way, Chiang could occupy smoothly all the territory then held by the Japanese. Also, with the assistance of Japanese troops, Chiang's forces would drive north, through the Communist areas, and secure Manchuria.

In return for this aid, Chiang would help the Japanese get a reasonable peace settlement from the Allies. He would also keep Japanese military and technical personnel as advisors; the Japanese would thus assure themselves of a military force and a General Staff, intact on the continent of Asia, after the war.

It was a deal that both sides needed. Chiang knew how weak his armies were, and how weak his government was. Although he had American support, he knew that support would not go so far as to help him militarily against the Communists. He needed the promise of Japanese help, because he knew a civil war with the Communists was just around the corner.

The immediate benefit to the Japanese was the gain of an ally at the peace table. In the longer term it was a way of preserving a substantial portion of their military strength and keeping a foothold on the mainland of China. The Japanese envisioned a Chinese-Japanese alliance that would one day emerge as a world power.

Exposure of the plan by the OSS in early 1945 doomed it to failure. But in any case it was a futile exercise, since the Allies were determined to accept nothing less than unconditional surrender from Germany and Japan. The very existence of a deal "cooking" between Chiang and the Japanese, however, was a revelation to Washington.

It was just part of the intelligence gathered by SI and X-2, under cover of the Dixie Mission into Communist-held China.

From the beginning of the OSS involvement in China, Gen. Donovan felt it essential to penetrate the Communist-held areas. The Nationalist leaders objected to any American contact with the Communists, but Gen. Donovan persisted. It was important that the OSS should gather intelligence on Japanese defenses and capabilities in northern China and important to measure the potential of the Communists as allies in the battle against Japan.

It was apparent that the Communists had liberated large areas of China from the Japanese and were doing a much better job of guerrilla fighting than the Nationalists. Gen. Donovan wanted to know why they were doing so well, how they were doing it, and whether or not the Communists would work with Americans against the Japanese.

On the highest levels in Washington opinion was divided on American contact with the Communist Chinese; within the State Department there was a conflict of ideas and support for both sides in China. For example, Vice-President Henry Wallace was in favor of Gen. Donovan's plan for the OSS contact. Patrick Hurley, the U.S. Ambassador to China, was apparently against it. Eventually, with the support of Wallace, who went to China to see for himself, a mission to Communist China was approved.

But the mission was not, officially at least, to have any

OSS agents with it. In July 1944, the mission, code-named Dixie, went to Yenan, the Communist capital. Nine men were in the July group and eleven more joined them in August. The Dixie Mission was headed by a Col. David D. Barrett, an Army Intelligence officer. There were also men from the 14th Air Force, 20th Bomber Command, the Office of War Information, the State Department—and the OSS, under cover of communications experts for 14th Air Force; Tai Li still refused permission for any OSS agents to enter Communist territory.

During the first eight months of the Dixie Mission, a certain amount of useful information was obtained by the OSS agents. This included details of Japanese strength in northern China, train counts on the rail lines connecting with southern China, weather reports for the Air Force, and information of Japanese espionage activities.

The political situation hampered OSS activity, however. Special Operations were forbidden. Chiang Kai-shek objected strongly to any material help or training for the Communists on the grounds that eventually they might be used against him in a civil war.

Some of the first reports out of Yenan by the OSS came from Capt. Charles C. Stelle and one of his associates, whose name has been eliminated from all reports out of China in official OSS files. According to Capt. Stelle, in a report dated August 7, 1944, "We are completely confident that it will be possible to secure thorough cooperation from the Chinese Communists for OSS operations. We have already secured informal assurances that the Communists will agree to our establishing independent communications and agents and that they will be glad to provide Chinese personnel for training in our methods . . ."

Capt. Stelle was guardedly optimistic. OSS agents, for diplomatic reasons previously mentioned, had to be careful to keep their cover as 14th Air Force men, or risk offending Chiang's government and Tai Li. Further, and for the same reasons, members of the Dixie Mission had permission only to "demonstrate" to the Communists, not to "instruct."

Thus Capt. Stelle reported later in August that "lectures" on the use of weapons and demolitions were given to some 500 officers and men of the 18th Group Army.

At the same time, an OSS report on the Chinese Communist overall situation was sent back to Washington. This is part of that report:

"The Eighth Route Army, New Fourth Army and affiliated forces have been carrying on the war of resistance in North, South and Central China for almost eight years, and the Kwantung East River guerrilla base under the same leadership has been carrying on the struggle in China for over six years.

"During this period their numbers have increased to 570,000 regulars, large numbers of guerrillas and auxiliary forces comprising 2,200,000 armed people's volunteers and home defense militia. These forces are supported by 90,000,000 people who comprise 45% of the entire population behind the Japanese lines . . ."

By November 1944 Capt. Stelle was reporting no progress, pending an agreement between Washington and Chiang Kai-shek on what the Dixie Mission could and could not do.

"From what we can see up here, however (reported

Capt. Stelle on Nov. 22, 1944), there seems to be some progress in at least bringing to a head the question of whether or not the United States is going to be able to exploit the undoubted military potentialities of the 18th Army Group. General Hurley, during his secret mission here, appeared to be impressed both by the military opportunities which are offered by the positions and capabilities of the 18th Group Army and by the reasonable nature of their demands vis-a-vis the Chinese Central Government. When he went back to Chungking he took with him Chou En-lai, #2 politico of the Communists, for negotiations with the Central Government, and a set of Communist terms for Communist-Central Government cooperation. It seems probable that Hurley himself will back up these terms . . ."

One month later, Lt. Col. Willis H. Bird, Deputy Chief of the OSS in China, visited Yenan, and in January 1945 sent a report to Gen. Wedemeyer and to Washington. Here are the main points of his report:

> All agreements made on Dixie Mission tentative and based on our government's approval of the project. Theater Command already agreed on principle of support to fullest extent of Communists and feel it is an OSS type project. If the government approves the following is tentative agreement:
>
> a. To place our S.O. men with their units for purposes of destroying Jap communications, air fields and blockhouses, and to generally raise hell and run . . .
>
> c. Points of attack to be selected in general by Wedemeyer. Details to be worked out in cooperation with Communists in that territory . . .

h. To receive complete cooperation of their army of six hundred fifty thousand and Peoples Militia of two and a half million when strategic use required by Wedemeyer . . .

The first meeting with Chu Teh was the morning of my arrival . . . After much discussion a meeting was called for the afternoon with the Chief of Staff . . . General Yeh . . .

Col. Bird went on in his report to talk of this meeting with Gen. Yeh and the problems both recognized in getting approval from Chiang Kai-shek for the plan. In conclusion, Col. Bird said:

"At the close of the talk the General stated regardless of whether we give them one rifle or one round of ammunition or not, the people of North China looked upon the United States as their best friend, and General Wedemeyer as their Commander-in-Chief, and would follow his military orders if he chose to give them."

But a stalemate followed these talks. To the OSS agents on the spot, it became obvious that Chiang Kai-shek would not budge in his stand against American cooperation with the Communists; he felt sure that no American government would support a Communist regime against an anti-Communist government, and, as became known later, he had the support of the Japanese against the Communists.

A report sent directly to Gen. Donovan in 1945 by OSS agents of the Dixie Mission summarized these problems and predicted that the mission would never get anywhere. This summary report is remarkable for its frankness. It is within this report that Chiang Kai-shek's plans for a deal with the Japanese are revealed. It was an extremely sensitive and secret report, and it is worth quoting the preamble to it verbatim, as well as its principal points:

> The following notes are based on information secured during the course of a six months stay in Yenan. Much of it is based on personal and completely unofficial statements from various Communist leaders. Some of it has been presented to American military authorities with the specific request that it not be made available to the American Ambassador (Author's note: that is, Gen. Patrick Hurley). Much of this information has been in theory made available to General Wedemeyer alone. It would be highly embarrassing, therefore, should the information contained in these notes reach non-OSS quarters.

> *Communist views on negotiations with*
> *the Central Government*

> 1. The Communists received General Hurley in Yenan, in early November, with a good deal of elation. General Hurley was the highest ranking American officer to visit Yenan and was the personal representative of the President. General Hurley's conversations in Yenan further bolstered the hopes of the Communists. In meetings with Mao Tse-tung and Chou En-lai a series of proposals were drafted which were to be the basis of negotiations with the Central Government. In general these proposals called for creation of a Coalition Government, recognition of the legality of minority parties, proportional distribution of military supplies, recognition of the validity of governments established under Communist aegis behind the Japanese lines, and,

as an earnest of good faith, immediate release of political prisoners.

The Communists state that General Hurley took an active part in drafting these proposals and that they were convinced that he would give the program his personal backing. When Hurley returned to Chungking, Chou En-lai accompanied him to carry on negotiations with the Generalissimo.

From the Communist point of view the negotiations in Chungking were unsatisfactory. Chiang did not see Chou En-lai for a considerable time and the interview was, according to Chou, so perfunctory as to be studiously insulting. The proposals which had been drafted in Yenan were met with a counter-proposal. Chiang suggested establishment of a Council, semi-executive, semi-advisory, in which the Communists together with the other minorities would be represented . . .

The Communists believed that the new Council would be too vague in function and too limited in power to have any value. They regarded the offer as a device by which Chiang intended to escape outright refusal of the Yenan program, a measure by which he could avoid real concessions without incurring the odium of obstructing negotiations . . .

Chou En-lai left Chungking, carrying Chiang's counter-proposal, ostensibly to consult with his party. Actually it was clear to Chou that the counter-proposal was so unsatisfactory to the Communists that further negotiations would be difficult if not impossible . . .

From that point on, the situation deteriorated rapidly. Gen. Hurley tried to get both sides together again, but he lost the confidence of the Communist leaders, accord-

ing to the OSS report. Mao and Chou felt he was being
fooled by Chiang with insincere proposals that were
meant to gain American sympathy, but give the Communists nothing. Further, they felt that Gen. Hurley was
being indiscreet, by giving information to Chiang that
they had given him, "in confidence."

In January 1945 Gen. Hurley asked Chou to come
once again to Chungking. The Communist inclination
was to refuse, since nothing had changed. But in order
to avoid appearing obstructive, Chou went. When he got
there he found one of the other minority parties in
China, the Federation of Democratic Parties, had already rejected Chiang's proposals.

Since the FDP was much less militant than the Communists, it was obvious to Chou that Chiang's proposals
would not be acceptable to him or his party. But he repeated, "unofficially [in the words of the OSS report]
that the Communists would still be willing to negotiate
on the basis of the original proposals which General
Hurley had assisted in drafting in Yenan, but that these
proposals were minimum and nothing else would be regarded as satisfactory . . ."

Mao and Chou were now thoroughly convinced that
Chiang would not accept a true coalition government or
give them any place at all in his government that had
any meaning. They also felt that Gen. Hurley no longer
fairly represented their case to his superiors. They sent a
message to Gen. Wedemeyer, the Theater Commander,
asking if it were possible for Mao or Chou or both to be
invited to Washington to meet President Roosevelt to
state their case. At the same time, they offered Gen.

Wedemeyer documentary proof of Chiang's dealings with the Japanese, as outlined earlier.

The OSS report continues with the Communist view on the balance of power in China. It stated that although the Communists feel they are stronger, both politically and militarily, than Chiang, they understood that he would not reach a settlement with them because he was confident of American and Japanese support.

Interestingly enough, according to the OSS report, "The Communists appear to have no particular disposition to quarrel with American diplomatic support for Chiang. Chiang, they say, has been recognized even by themselves as the President of China and naturally should be regarded as such by the American Government.

"Nor have the Communists been disturbed by the American policy of making support for themselves contingent upon a political agreement with the Central Government, although they now state that since these negotiations have failed, and since it is—to them—apparent that the Central Government is not going to make a settlement it is up to the United States to decide whether or not it will now reconsider this policy . . ."

By spring, the Dixie Mission was just about ready to fold. In a report to Col. Richard P. Heppner, a senior OSS officer in China, Capt. Stelle refers to the "Impasse in Dixie," and spells out Communist disappointment with American policy. By now Gen. Hurley, back in Washington, fully supported Chiang and stated that no arms should be given the Communists.

The Communists pointed out to Capt. Stelle that they had never asked for arms, but did resent the fact that America was equipping fresh divisions for Chiang which would not be used against the Japanese, but against them. Yet it was they who represented the only effective fighting force against the Japanese.

Under the heading, "Crystal Ball, Yenan Variety," Capt. Stelle reported, "What Yenan wants right now is very apparent. The Communists want to know whether there is any chance that the present policy of full support for Chungking alone is subject to modification. They want to know what American military policy will be if the U.S. Army lands or comes into their areas. They want to know what they can expect to get in the way of concrete military benefit from American operations in these areas . . .

"The Communists state freely that the Dixie Mission has benefited them in a propaganda way, but . . . latest policy so far as the Communists can see, is full support for their enemies and no support for themselves . . ."

In June and July the Dixie Mission was withdrawn. In July all OSS activities in Communist China were ended, as it became apparent that the war with Japan would soon end, and when it did, a civil war would break out in China.

With hindsight, a reading of the OSS reports on both China and Indochina would seem to indicate that the United States backed the wrong horses in Asia. But the subject of American policy in Asia is not as simple as that.

What does appear certain from the OSS reports, however, is that for many years the American public was at best ill-informed, and at worst, misinformed, of the progress of events in Asia on the political battlefront.

EPILOGUE

The strongest efforts of the OSS were quite naturally directed toward those areas where United States forces were, or would be, involved in the heaviest combat. But while agents concentrated on Secret Intelligence and Special Operations in the heart of Europe and in Japanese-occupied Asia, OSS units were also at work in the outlying areas. OSS joined British services in helping resistance movements in Greece, Albania, Yugoslavia, Czechoslovakia, Denmark, and Norway. The British worked almost alone in the field in Belgium, Holland, and Poland, but here, too, they were backed up by OSS Special Operations officers in London, who helped with planning, training, and communications.

OSS spies were sent all over Africa and Turkey and to various countries of the Middle East. Their purpose was to counter the activities of the Germans in those areas. Remote ports were being used as refueling depots for U-boats, for the smuggling of vital war materials to Germany, for spying on Allied shipping.

The guerrilla activities of the Special Operations teams in these outlying areas were duly rewarding. Tens of thousands of German troops which could have been used in France or Italy against the Allies were instead pinned down fighting the resistance and guarding important installations.

According to OSS estimates, some forty German divisions were thus diverted. Troop casualties numbered in the thousands; the morale of German soldiers in the remoter garrison areas was badly affected. Supplies never reached their destinations. Factories in Norway and Denmark closed down or produced faulty war material, deliberately sabotaged.

In Greece and in Yugoslavia, where partisan activity was particularly strong, the OSS again encountered political problems, often disagreeing with British policy. In both countries partisan forces were split between the Communists and the rightist groups. In Greece a civil war between the royalists and the Communists erupted at the end of 1944, while World War II was still in progress. The presence of OSS agents in the area provided the United States government with inside information on the warring groups.

In Yugoslavia there was a similar problem, as the Russian-backed forces of Marshal Tito fought not only the Germans, but the Chetniks under Gen. Mihailovich. Here, too, in view of today's power struggles in the world, it is interesting to note that, according to OSS reports, Tito, though certainly a Communist, and certainly backed by Russia, fought a genuine battle against the Nazis. On the other hand, it is equally clear that Mihailovich joined forces with the Nazis in an attempt to wipe out Tito's partisans and further his own ambitions.

Much of this information on Yugoslavia was rather

late in getting through to both British and American leaders. Since Mihailovich was connected with the Yugoslav Royal Family in exile, the tendency was to support him and his Chetniks. Indeed, in the United States, he and his Chetniks were glorified as heroes. This country was still rather naive when it came to the intrigues and intricacies of Balkan politics. We tended to follow the British lead or put our faith in existing institutions.

As the war moved into late 1943 and 1944, however, OSS reports from Yugoslavia and from neutral capitals began to paint a different picture. The British, too, began to catch on to the fact that regardless of Tito's political leanings, he was fighting the enemies of the Allies, while Mihailovich was maneuvering for Mihailovich.

One of the first OSS reports on Chetnik collaboration with the Germans came in a secret memorandum dated May 5, 1943. It identifies certain Yugoslavs organizing Chetnik forces to fight on the side of the Italians and the Germans against the Allies. Said the memorandum: "The chief organizer of those chetniks was Ilja Trifunovich-Birchanin, a friend of General Drazha Mihailovich . . ."

A follow-up secret memorandum dated May 25–26, 1943, reports an enemy offensive building up against the Tito partisans, using eight German and three Italian divisions. The report also identifies 15,000 Chetniks armed by the Germans and Italians, joining them against the partisans.

Nonetheless, the United States position was still divided. Two months after the receipt of these reports in Washington, two Special Operations officers flew out of Cairo and were parachuted into Yugoslavia, one to join

Tito, one to join Mihailovich. Each agent sent reports favoring the group to which he was attached and attacking the opposite group. However, the evidence on Mihailovich's support for the Nazis was overwhelming. In early 1944, all U.S. and British support for Mihailovich was withdrawn.

But American airmen continued to bail out over Chetnik territory, where there were no longer OSS agents to help them and get them back home. Further, there was high-level pressure to maintain intelligence sources all over Yugoslavia, especially since Tito, while friendly, was a Communist. Support for a renewed OSS liaison with Mihailovich came principally from Ambassador Robert D. Murphy, and Air Force Generals Eaker and Twining.

On August 3, 1944, a three-man team, codenamed Halyard, parachuted to Pranjane, near Belgrade, where Mihailovich had collected 250 American airmen. The Halyard team hired 300 laborers and built an air strip in one week. When it was completed a fleet of C-47 transports flew in and evacuated the airmen. Team Halyard remained in the area until November 1944, helping to evacuate a total of 400 men.

Meantime, late in August, a six-man intelligence mission had parachuted in. It proved to be a dreadful mistake. By now Tito was more or less recognized as the head of the Yugoslav government; the British had established diplomatic relations with him. The chief of the American intelligence group, a lt. colonel, explained to Mihailovich that his assignment was purely to collect intelligence and that his visit in no way implied support for the Chetniks.

But Mihailovich, still fighting for his political life, turned the occasion to his advantage. A few days after the mission's arrival there appeared a leaflet, in the Serbo-Croatian language, saying:

". . . The delegates of the Allied American Government and the personal representatives of President Roosevelt, the tried friend of freedom loving nations, have arrived.

"Immediately, upon his arrival, Colonel _____ (deleted by OSS) and the members of his mission went to the headquarters of the Supreme Command. On this occasion he presented a written message from President Roosevelt . . ."

This was, of course, an outright lie. But the effect was precisely what Mihailovich hoped for. Tito was enraged and immediately stopped cooperating with British and American liaison officers. OSS reports carefully point out, however, that Tito might well have been looking for some excuse to stop working with the Allies, since the Russians were now approaching. Be that as it may, relations with Tito remained cool after that incident. In October 1944 a new independent American Military Mission to Marshal Tito arrived in Yugoslavia and took command of all U.S. teams there. A few weeks later the Mihailovich team was withdrawn. But by now the Russians were fighting the Germans in Belgrade, and Tito's allegiance was committed.

With the experience gained by the OSS during World War II, the seeds were sown for a permanent U.S. intelligence organization. Immediately after the end of hostilities, however, President Harry Truman disbanded the

OSS. This took place via an Executive Order of October 1, 1945.

The OSS officially died on that day, but unofficially, operating under various covers and on the payrolls of various government departments, former OSS agents worked on. They remained in such politically sensitive and unstable areas as China, Vietnam, India, Laos, Thailand, Cambodia, the Philippines, Korea, Greece, Turkey, Yugoslavia, the Mideast, and in much of Europe.

Though he disbanded the OSS, President Truman did see the need for a permanent, central U.S. intelligence operation. Had the United States such an organization in 1941, he stated, there could never have been a Pearl Harbor.

He therefore passed through Congress the National Security Act of 1947, establishing the Central Intelligence Agency. Truman originally envisioned an agency in the prewar Coordinator of Information role, as an intelligence-gathering organization, operating openly. But the old hands from the OSS saw beyond that concept, to an organization that would show just the tip of the iceberg, but operate clandestinely to further the political aims of the United States.

Gen. Donovan saw the CIA in that light. So did Allen Dulles and such former OSS operatives as William Colby and Frank Wisner. Eventually, in 1949, the Central Intelligence Agency Act was passed, giving the CIA wide scope for covert activities, under the direction of the National Security Council. Dulles, mastermind of the OSS Bern station, became first chief of the CIA's Clandestine Services. Later, he became Director of the entire CIA.

BIBLIOGRAPHY

Causes, Origins, and Lessons of the Vietnam War. Washington, D.C.: U.S. Government Printing Office, 1973.

Cookridge, E. H. *Inside S.O.E.* London: Arthur Barker, Ltd., 1966.

Dulles, Allen. *The Secret Surrender.* New York: Harper & Row, 1966.

Farago, Ladislas. *Burn After Reading.* New York: Mac-Fadden, 1963.

FitzGibbon, Constantine. *Secret Intelligence in the Twentieth Century.* London: Hart-Davis, MacGibbon, 1976.

Foot, M. R. D. *S.O.E. in France.* London: Her Majesty's Stationery Office, 1966.

Macksey, Kenneth. *The Partisans of Europe in the Second World War.* New York: Stein and Day, 1975.

Rowan, Richard Wilmer, and Deindorfer, Robert G. *Secret Service: 33 Centuries of Espionage.* New York: Hawthorn, 1967.

Schellenberg, Walter. *The Schellenberg Memoirs.* London: André Deutch, 1963.

Shirer, William L. *The Rise and Fall of the Third Reich.* New York: Simon & Schuster, 1960.

INDEX

ABOUT THE AUTHOR

Milton J. Shapiro was born and raised in Brooklyn, New York. He went to Boys High School there, and then to the College of the City of New York. Two years in the Army, including a year with the 13th Air Force in the Philippines, interrupted his college education. Resuming at CCNY, Mr. Shapiro was graduated with a BBA and served as Features Editor of *Ticker*, the college newspaper. While still a senior at CCNY, he joined a daily newspaper as copy boy, rose to sports writer, and then film critic. Later, he switched his writing and editing to magazines, directing the publishing activities of several different companies. He authored many sports biographies for young people until moving to London, England, several years ago. For a time he worked with Reuters, the British news agency, and was publishing director for the British branch of Warner Communications, Inc. Now married to an English woman, he is a freelance writer of paperback books, books for young people, and magazine articles.